The Lives And Times Of Our English Ancestors

Volume 2

Frank Smith, F. S. G.

The Everton Publishers
P.O. Box 368 - Logan, Utah 84321

Printed by

Keith W. Watkins and Sons, Inc.
Providence. Utah 84332

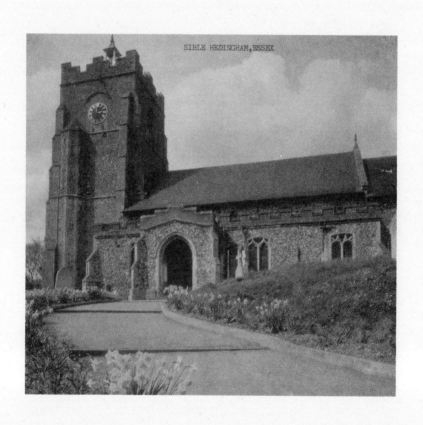

SIBLE HEDINGHAM, ESSEX

III

WELFORD ON AVON, WARWICKSHIRE

IV

LITTLE BADDOW, ESSEX

V

History is every man's story, the road along which man came. Seek it wherever you are, striking down roots that will nourish and strengthen you. For only by knowing of yesterday can today and tomorrow have meaning, only then do we keep our perspective, only then do we steady our aim.

-Family History

For some people the past is not only dead but was never alive; its people figments of a schoolmarm's imagination, its records as expendable as a packet of cigarettes.

-Author Unknown

CONTENTS

PREFACE

Volume 1 of *Lives and Times of Our English Ancestors* re-created the past in a series of short chapters, one for each century, 1100 to 1900 A.D. It was meant as a broad overview of the conditions under which our ancestors lived, emphasizing in general terms only the economic conditions under which our poorer ancestors lived.

Today, it is being recognized more and more that history is people--their actions and reactions, their physical circumstances, their employment, how they ate and clothed themselves. The history of an ancestor is not only who he was, but also what he did, what happened to him; and what happened to him was often determined by the circumstances with which he was surrounded.

This volume deals largely with actual events that took place in the lives of persons or groups of persons, representing, in the social strata, the more than 90% of the population, the lower classes. Unlike Volume 1, this volume deals with only four centuries, 1500-1900. 1500 was chosen as the earliest date because prior to that time, the records are not as numerous and the chances of extending a working class pedigree prior to that year are very low.

I have placed more emphasis in this volume on our working class ancestors because so much has already been written about the wealthier ones, yet everyone has ancestors in the lower classes about whom not enough has been written.

Admittedly, I am partial to the humbler class because I was a child in a coal-mining family. My sisters were among the tens of thousands who worked long hours "downstairs" as domestic servants under conditions that are not tolerated today.

What is amazing to me is that the conditions described in this volume were pretty much taken for granted except for an occasional uprising which was quickly squashed. Today we wish our own children could come up the hard way and learn the valuable lessons we learned. The next best thing is to make sure they know some of the experiences we and our ancestors had so that they can appreciate all our modern day blessings.

Unlike volume 1, this volume is also designed to help you in writing your multi-generation English family history. The last two chapters show how such a family history can be written, drawing from a wide variety of documents and background material. Perhaps in no other country is there such a wide variety of documents available for personal and family histories regardless of the economic circumstances of our ancestors.

Chances that your individual ancestor is actually named in the following pages is slight. But the same things or similar things could have happened to him so you will be able to relate these same events to the people from whom you descended.

I have a personal conviction that we shall meet these people again. There will be time to swap stories. I think we will listen with awe and admiration as we listen to each others' life story. Consider this volume, then, a prelude to that time.

ACKNOWLEDGEMENTS

As with volume 1 of this series, I wish to thank Thomas Hope and Sankey Hudson of Manchester, England for their unqualified permission to reproduce material from their publications:

The Story of Prehistoric and Roman Britain Told in Pictures,

The Story of Saxon and Norman Britain Told in Pictures,

The Story of Medieval Britain Told in Pictures,

The Story of Tudor and Stuart Britain Told in Pictures,

The Story of Hanoverian and Modern Britain Told in Pictures-

all authored by C. W. Airne, M.A., and also *Britain's Story Told in Pictures.*

Additional thanks to Adam and Charles Black, Publishers, of London, England for permission to use illustrations from their publication *Occupational Costumes in England* (Cunnington and Lucas).

I also wish to thank Evans Brothers of London, England, for use of material in their *Kingsway History* series, and to all others whose works have been referred to in the text.

Encourage your local library to purchase copies of these books, or buy them for your own library.

There are many hours of good reading to be found in a large number of books and they will prove far more interesting than many of today's television programs. No bibliography has been prepared since there are literally hundreds of books that pertain to our English ancestors. To know which to include and which to leave out of a bibliography would be almost impossible.

For example I recently completed reading a book

titled *For the Term of His Natural Life,* by Marcus Clarke (Oxford University Press, 1952). It begins with the circumstances surrounding a crime that was committed, the wrong party charged with the crime, the convict ship experience to Australia, his escapes and captures, the conditions under which the captives lived. Tens of thousands went to Australia under similar circumstances. If one of these so-called convicts was an ancestor then this is a useful book to read.

HISTORICAL	RELIGIOUS	RECORD-KEEPING	SOCIAL, ECONOMICAL
1509 HENRY THE EIGHTH (1509-47).	ca. 1510 Early years of the English Renaissance or "New Learning."		
1512 War with France. 1513 Battles of the Spurs and of Flodden Field.			
1520 Field of the Cloth of Gold.	ca. 1521 Early years of the English Reformation.		
1522 War with France.	1523 Tyndale's English version of the Bible secretly distributed.		Increased national prosperity and commerce with foreign countries.
1534-35 Henry VIII assumed the title of Supreme Head of the Church of England.	1534 English renunciation of papal supremacy. 1534-38 Suppression of first the lesser and then the greater monasteries.	1536 First attempts to initiate the keeping of parish registers failed.	
1536-38 Rebellions in the northern counties against the suppression of the monasteries.		1538 Parish registers ordered to be kept; registers successfully initiated.	
1544 War with France. 1547 EDWARD THE SIXTH (1547-53).	ca. 1550 Walloon Protestants arrive as refugees from the Low Countries	1547 The injunction to keep parish registers reiterated.	
1533 MARY (1553-58).	1553-58 Queen Mary promoted Catholicism. Protestants persecuted and many burned at the stake.	1553 Many parish ministers replaced by those favoring the queen.	
1558 War with France, loss of Calais. 1558 ELIZABETH THE FIRST (1558-1603).	1559 Reorganization of the Church of England settled moderately.	1558 Injunction reinforcing the keeping of parish registers.	New trading companies were established.

THE SIXTEENTH CENTURY

HISTORICAL	RELIGIOUS	RECORD-KEEPING	SOCIAL, ECONOMICAL
1560 War with Scotland.	1560 Calvinism made the national religion of Scotland.		Literature and learning greatly advanced; new universities and grammar schools were founded.
1562 African slave trade commenced.	1563 Papal recusants heavily fined for nonattendance at church. The Test Act excluded Roman Catholics from governmental office.	1567 Earliest date in the French Protestant and Walloon registers.	The Statute of Apprentices of 1563 tried to regulate wages and employment.
	1571-72 Presbyterianism introduced into England by Thomas Cartwright.		
1579 Act of Uniformity in matters of religion enforced	1580-81 Robert Browne, an early Separatist from the Church of England, established a Separatist church in Norwich. His followers, "Brownists," later were known as Independents or Congregationalists.	1578 Earliest date in the Quaker (or Society of Friends) Records.	
1584 Virginia first colonized.	1592 A congregational (or Independent) church was formed in London.		
1588 Defeat of the Spanish Armada.	1593 The Conventicle Act aimed against the preaching and worship of Nonconformists.		
1597 Revolt in Ireland		1597 All parish registers ordered to be copied on parchment. A copy to be sent to the bishop's office annually.	

Chapter One

THE SIXTEENTH CENTURY

Like as the waves make towards the pebbled shore,
So do our minutes hasten to their end;
Each changing place with that which goes before
In sequent toil all forwards do contend.
Nativity, once in the main of light,
Crawls to maturity, wherewith being crown'd,
Crooked eclipses 'gainst his glory fight,
And Time that gave doth now his gift confound.
Time doth transfix the flourish set on youth,
And delves the parallels in beauty's brow,
Feeds on the rarities of nature's truth,
And nothing stands but for his scythe to mow.
And yet to times in hope my verse shall stand,
Praising thy worth, despite his cruel hand.

William Shakespeare, Sonnet LX

A glimpse of England as it was in the century when records for common people began to be made in reasonable quantities is worthwhile, not only for its own sake but also as an introduction to life in later centuries.

The sixteenth century marked the end of the Middle Ages and the beginning of the modern age. In sixteenth-century England, less than half the land was under cultivation. There were large wooded areas, and the fens of East Anglia were still undrained. The population lived mostly in a large number of small villages. Apart from these small towns, there was only one large town--London--and only two main ports--London and Bristol.

Living conditions depended somewhat on the topography of the area. In the less hilly areas the manorial system, in which the lord of the manor owned the land and hired several classes of workers, still flourished, although the change to an open-field system was slowly taking place.

In some instances, of course, your ancestor might have been the lord of the manor. In other instances he may have been lucky enough to be a freeman, free to work his own land and to help the lord only at harvest time. The villeins and bordars were unfree tenants. They had to work several days each week for the lord of the manor and look after their own strips of land in the remaining days. The cottars had no strips of land of their own except the cottage garden. They worked full time for the manorial lord. The

3

✦

bordars, the lowest class of all, were practically slaves.

Farmers were yet to learn how to grow good crops in quantity. At harvest time the lord's crops had to be gathered first. It is only fair to say, however, that in most instances the manor was operated in a very democratic manner. Even the lord could be chastized at the manor court (usually held monthly) if fences needed repair or if there was some other problem affecting life on the manorial estate.

Although changes were taking place in the manorial system, it persisted in some areas for several more centuries.

Manor court rolls are an extremely valuable source for genealogical research, providing background information for individuals living on the manorial estate. The following adventures of one John Rayner are recorded in *The Common Stream: Portrait of an English Village for 2,000 Years,* by Rowland Parker (New York: Holt, Rinehart and Winston, 1975). He must have been one big headache to Foxton (Huntingdonshire) Manor Court.

1541. He refused to appear with others to enquire into the unlawful lengthening of a hedge; fined 12*d*.
1543. He encroached with his plough on various balks in various places; fined 4*d*.
1550. He was ordered to mend the fence between him and Bartholomew Mathewson.
He encroached with his plough at Whytmoreshot; fined 4*d*.
1551. He assaulted Richard Day and drew blood; fined . . .
1553. He enclosed part of the public way with a wall; fined 12*d*.
1554. He was ordered to remove the hedge between him and Mathewson.
1558. He failed to widen a drain as ordered; fined 4*d*.
He failed to repair a hedge next to John Kyng; fined 3*s* 4*d*.
He kept a dog which was in the habit of worrying sheep; fined 3*d*.
1559. He trespassed on the land of Will Fuller and did damage to the extent of 6*s* 8*d*.
He trespassed and did damage on the land of John Kyng to the extent of 10*s*.
1561. He occupied ½ acre of enclosed pasture without title.
He was ordered to mend the fences between him and John Calcott.
He was ordered to mend the fences between him and Elena King.
1562. He ploughed up the common balks; fined 12*d*.
He was ordered to mend the fences next to John Smith.
1566. He removed the common boundary-marks in the fields; fined 12*d*.
He cut branches from two willow trees of Agnes Crosse; fined 3*s* 4*d*.
He was ordered to replace boundary-marks in Hayditch Shott.
1568. He was ordered to repair the fence at Andrews; fined 12*d*.
He failed to clean out the ditch there; fined 12*d*.
He made a ditch somewhere else; fined 6*d*.
He encroached on 5 roods of Trinity land in Chawdwell Felde; fined 12*d*.
He set a bad example by taking the oath negligently in court; fined 12*d*.

1571. He encroached on manor land at Andrews and stole a tree; fined 20*d*.
1576. He encroached on the road-way in Woodway Shott; fined 12*d*.
He ploughed over a boundary in Woodway Shott to the extent of one furrow; fined 12*d*.

He encroached with his plough at the Shot, using his fork, at Flag Pyghtell; fined 3s 4d.

He ploughed and encroached on a balk-end; fined 12d.

He failed to amend the encroachment at Andrews; fined 10s.

He trespassed when mowing upon the manor land of Richard Fuller to the extent of a swathe and half; fined 2s.

He ploughed 5 roods in Downfield contrary to orders; fined 2s.

1578. He was ordered to mend the fences between him and Thomas Wells.

1581. He let loose his beasts at Apletons; fined 12d.

He lopped two willows of John Fuller; fined 4d.

1586. He was ordered to mend the fence between him and Perrys.

The animals your sixteenth-century ancestors knew were of a smaller variety than those we know today. Their main use was for skins rather than for meat. Deer and wild boar roamed through the forests in large numbers but were not to be killed at will by the common peasant.

Meat was salted down in order to last through the winter and spring. Very often this meat was not properly cured and was the cause of scurvy and a contributor to the frequent plagues. This was to change with the introduction of root crops, mainly turnips, which allowed animals to be fed through the winter months.

Villagers never traveled very far from home since to do so usually meant they had to walk. The farthest most of them got was to the market, when the farmer needed help taking his produce.

During the sixteenth century your working ancestors woke up to a number of surprises. Whereas the century had started well for them--plenty of food, reasonable security on the manors--suddenly they found themselves with a debased coinage worth only one-third its previous value. With the dissolution of the monasteries by Henry VIII, many were without employment. Those members of country gilds who looked forward to retiring with a pension suddenly found that the king and noblemen had seized the funds and that they had now lost their protection from sickness and want. One could hardly imagine a thing like that happening today; but at that time the country people could not read or write, so the management of county and national affairs was left to a relative few.

On some other morning your ancestors may have awakened to find that the lands of the manor were being enclosed and divided among several of the more wealthy in the area who could earn more from the land by raising sheep. This movement toward enclosure was gradual but created much unemployment for those who did not have any money to buy land. Now they had to give up the common pasture where they could raise pigs and cows and try to find work elsewhere as farm laborers.

Thus was created a large band of "sturdy beggars," who not only begged but stole. With no police force, shutters went up very quickly when such bands arrived in the town or village. One such band was a cause of the uprising in Norwich in 1549 known as Kett's rebellion, which resulted in the death of Kett and one thousand of his followers. Persistent beggars and thieves were branded.

Such practices seem brutal in the twentieth century, but these were facts of life which you must understand if you are to appreciate your heritage.

A Horde of Beggars Invading a Town
From an Engraving by Weidetz, 1535

Much is said about your coal-mining ancestors in the chapter on nineteenth-century life, but some of us had coal-mining ancestors much earlier than the 1800s. The Romans mention that coal was washed up by the tide (hence it was first known as "sea cole"). There is reference to coal being used in small quanitites in the thirteenth century, and by the sixteenth century there were many small coal mines.

At this early date your coal-mining ancestors are reported to have been in a state of complete serfdom. Those in the north of England and in Scotland were bound for life, this slavelike condition persisting into the eighteenth century. Much has been written lately about the Negro slave trade, but there were many similar conditions among whites in Europe that were just as tragic.

Children working in a coal mine. The Exploitation of child labour was the worst feature of industrial development.

Tudor vagrants. Unemployment was a grave social problem. It was solved by the Elizabethan Poor Law, 1601.

HUNDRED *of* STAPLOW, MIDDLESEX. SEAL USED FOR LABOURERS' PASSES.

KETT'S OAK OF REFORMATION, WYMONDHAM.

KIRTON PARISH CHURCH, LINCOLNSHIRE

AMBERLEY CHURCH, SUSSEX

To fully appreciate the lives of your English ancestors, you must first understand the parish church, for it was there that almost all life--social as well as religious--centered. And what is true about the parish church in the sixteenth century is true for all four centuries discussed in this book.

The church was usually made of local stone, although some churches made of local rock and a few even made of wood can still be seen. It probably had a tower--either round or square--to house the bells, and it may have had a steeple. It was often a place of refuge against storms or civil disturbances, which accounts in part for its thick walls and narrow windows. Part of the church may have been built in Saxon times, or it may have had a Norman tower; but if it is still standing most of it has probably been rebuilt several times over.

Most parish churches have had short accounts written about them, often available at a very small cost at the churches themselves. For the background of parish churches in general, read *How to Study an Old Church,* by A. Needham (London: Batsford, 1944).

Inside, usually near the main entrance at the west end of the church was the baptismal font. Fonts have changed in size and design over the years, but all were used for the sprinkling of children in arms. They stood several feet off the floor and were made of stone, variously decorated and hollowed out at the top to hold the holy water.

Most churches had chancel screens, beautifully carved in oak. In smaller churches there would usually be only one separating the altar from the congregation.

The rood (an image of Christ on the cross) was fixed above the chancel screen on a rood beam. Many were destroyed during the Reformation, when zealous reformers attempted to simplify the church.

The altar was beyond the chancel screen and always at the east end of the church. It was here that the priest and his assistant prepared the sacrament. Most churches now have the pulpit near the congregation, but at one time the sermon was given from in front of the altar. Anciently, the congregation stood during the whole service, but by the sixteenth century pews or benches had been erected for the congregation. Often there was a special pew for the squire (who owned most of the land and, together with the parish priest, was the most important person in the village), his family, and, sometimes the servants too. Other influential people in the parish could pay to have their own pew, where no one else was allowed to sit.

During the Reformation most organs were destroyed, and galleries were built to house a group of musicians. Organs were restored in the eighteenth century. Your own ancestor could have worked as a carpenter on the beautiful woodwork, a stonemason on the walls, a bell ringer, a gardener for the parish priest, a grave digger, a parish clerk, an organist, a churchwarden, or a member of the vestry.

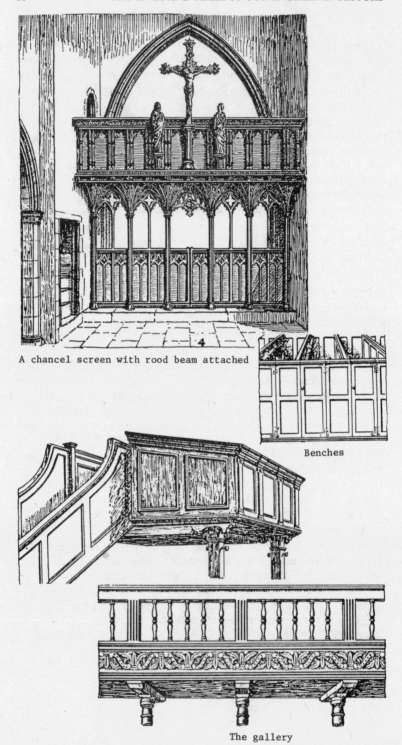

A chancel screen with rood beam attached

Benches

The gallery

If the parish church was the heart of sixteenth-century life, then the church bells were the voice. They called your ancestors to church on Sundays, celebrated Christmas, rang in the new year, opened fairs, announced marriages, warned of an advancing enemy or invasion, and warned of floods or, in the Fens, of the breaking of a dyke. At the funerals of some of your ancestors, they tolled the age of the deceased. In some churches to this day the bells play tunes at frequent intervals, every three or four hours. And even today there is little more beautiful on a summer day out in the country than to hear in the distance peals from the bells in the tower of the parish church.

In all countries many legends have surrounded church bells. They were supposed to ease the pain of pregnant women and to ward off the witches and devils that in your ancestors' day seemed very real.

Many of the bells have Latin transcriptions which, translated, say such things as:

"May the Festal Lamb be near at hand, that He may of his goodness put plagues to flight."

"I drive away pestilence."

"With my voice I praise the Lord for pestilence vanished."

The special significance church bells had for your ancestors can be seen in the following poem by Longfellow:

> The bells themselves are the best of preachers,
> Their brazen lips are learned teachers,
> From their pulpits of stone, in the upper air,
> Sounding aloft without crack or flaw,
> Shriller than trumpets under the law,
> Now a sermon, and now a prayer;
> The clangorous hammer is the tongue,
> This way, that way, beaten and swung,
> That from mouth of brass, as from mouth of gold,
> Might be taught the testaments, new and old.
> And above it the great cross beam of wood
> Representeth the Holy Rood,
> Upon which, like the bell, our hopes are hung.
> And the wheel wherewith it is swayed and swung
> Is the mind of man, that round and round
> Sways and maketh the tongue to sound!
> And the rope, with its twisted cordage three,
> Denoteth the Scriptural Trinity
> Of Morals, and Symbols, and History;
> And the upward and downward motions show
> That we touch upon matters high and low;
> And the constant change and transmutation
> Of action and of contemplation,
> Downward, the Scripture brought from on high.
> Upward, exalted again to the sky;
> Downward, the literal interpretation,
> Upward, the vision and mystery.

'BIG BEN' the great bell of Westminster. Cast at the Whitechapel foundry April 10. 1858.

In our modern day it may be very hard to understand the importance our ancestors placed on bells. A passage concerning the two pilgrims in John Bunyan's famous *Pilgrim's Progress* may help:

> *They had the City itself in view, and they thought they heard all the bells therein to ring to welcome them thereto . . . Now I saw in my dream, that these two men went in at the gate, and lo, as they entered, they were transfigured; and they had raiment put on that shone like gold. There were also that met them with harps and crowns in token of honour. They I heard in my dream that all the bells in the City rang out again for joy, and that it was said unto them, "Enter ye into the joy of your Lord."*

For several centuries, tithes were paid in kind to the parish minister, so a building, called a tithe barn, had to be built close to the parish church.

Also not far from the church there was usually an inn, where travelers could put up for the night.

Today the parish church seems the symbol of tranquility. But in the sixteenth century it was a battleground for a religious struggle that was to affect the faith of Englishmen for centuries. The century was only one-third gone when Henry VIII announced his historic break with the Catholic church and established the Church of England, with himself at the head.

During his short reign, Edward VI continued the religious policy of his father, Henry. The heresy acts were repealed and the English prayer books issued. But when Edward's half-sister Mary succeeded him in 1553, the break with Rome was reversed. England again acknowledged the pope, the heresy acts were revived, and those who refused to accept these changes were persecuted.

Henry VIII., 1509-47. Enlightened, accomplished and popular. Notable for his despotic rule and his advanced foreign and religious policies.

These turbulent times produced many martyrs, both Catholic and Protestant. You are descended from persons who lived their religion with a fierce zeal. For this, many of them paid with their lives, sometimes after years of prison and torture. The following story of a young man who was martyred for his religious beliefs at the age of nineteen, leaving no descent, was recorded by his brother Robert and appeared in Foxe's *Book of Martyrs,* published in 1570.

William Hunter was born in Brentwood in 1536, and was apprenticed to a silk weaver, Thomas Tailor, in London. By this time, the pendulum had swung in favor of Catholicism. In the atmosphere of religious zeal, it is understandable that when William refused to receive the communion at a mass he was dismissed by his master.

****

One day some time later, in Brentwood Chapel, he was reading the English Bible, a copy of which Henry VIII had ordered to be placed in every church. Here he was seen by Father Atwell, who already suspected him because he knew why he had returned home. Accordingly, Father Atwell fetched the chaplain of the chapel, Thomas Wood, who was also vicar of South Weald. He is described as being "in an alehouse even over against the said Chapel."

****

These two proceeded to question William about the meanings of certain passages in the Bible. His answers showed he denied the doctrine of transubstantiation, which is that at the communion the bread and wine are actually changed into the body and blood of Christ. William believed that he received the bread and wine in memory of the Lord. This was regarded as heresy, and so began his road to martyrdom.

****

Thomas Wood immediately reported the conversation to the local justice, Antony Browne, who in 1554 had been appointed a commissioner to enforce the Statute of Heretics. Not wanting to be responsible for the terrible fate in store for William if he were convicted of heresy, Browne did his best to save the lad. He pointed out that in St. Luke, Chapter 22, Christ said that the bread was his body, but William argued that this was meant merely as figure of speech and was not intended to be taken literally. Browne became infuriated at the youth's stubbornness and sent him to the bishop of London, Bishop Bonner.

****

Bishop Bonner was usually ruthless towards those who opposed him, but he evidently liked William from the start and did all he could to get him to recant. At first he tried persuasion, and, when this failed, force. He had the youth put in the stocks for two days and two nights, with only a crust of bread and a cup of water; and when this had no effect he had him sent to a convict prison and put in irons. During the nine months he was there, the bishop tried five more times to persuade him to go back on what he had said, but William consistently refused. Accordingly, on February 9, 1555, he, with five others, was condemned in the consistory court at St. Paul's. The sentence was the he should go to Newgate, and thence to Brentwood to be burned at the stake.

****

Even after this the bishop made a last attempt to save William, this time by bribery, offering to make him a free-man in the city and give him money to set himself up, or to make him a steward in his own house. William still remained steadfast to what he believed to be the right interpretation of the Lord's word, saying, "If you cannot persuade my conscience with scriptures, I cannot find it in my heart to turn from God for the love of the world."

****

He was therefore taken, with the others condemned at the same time, to Newgate, and about a month later to Brent-wood. He arrived at Brentwood on Saturday, March 23, and stayed at the Swan Inn, then in the High Street. Monday was the Feast of the Annunciation of the Blessed Virgin Mary, so there were no burnings on that day. During this time William was visted by his father and mother, who, instead of upbraid-ing him for his stubbornness, praised him for being true to his faith. On Monday night he dreamt of the scene of the martyr-dom, just as it was the following day.

****

When that day, Tuesday, March 26, dawned, the sheriff, Edward Brockett, called on the people to "set forward to the burning of William Hunter." William showed no fear, and when Brockett's son went to comfort him he said: "I thank God I am not afraid. I have cast my count what it will cost me already." He came out of the Swan Inn, the sheriff's servant taking one arm and Robert, his brother, the other; and the pathetic procession with priests, the sheriff and other officials, soldiers "with bows, bills and weapons," and local people made its way up the High Street "to the place where the stake stood."

****

There William knelt down and read the fifty-first Psalm. The chain was made fast. He said, "Son of God, shine upon me," whereupon "immediately the sun in the element shone out of a dark cloud so full in his face that he was constrained to look another way, whereat the people mused, because it was so dark a little time afore."

Finally William pressed his psalter into his brother's hand. Robert said, "William, think on the holy passion of Christ, and be not afraid of death," to which William replied, "I am not afraid."

He lifted up his hands to heaven as he spoke his last words: "Lord, Lord, receive my spirit." And "casting down his head again into the smothering smoke he yielded up his life for the truth, sealing it with his blood, to the praise of God."

The following incident, recorded in Foxe's *Act and Monuments*, vol. 3, shows a very unusual approach by the sheriff as thirteen martyrs, eleven men and two women, prepare to meet their fate:

On the morning of their martyrdom at Stratford-le-Bow, June 27th, 1556, "the thirteen were divided into two parts in two separate chambers, and the Sheriff came to the one part and told them that the other had recanted, and their lives should be saved if they did so. But they replied, that their faith was not builded on man, but on Christ crucified. Then the Sheriff, perceiving he could not influence them, went to the other part and said the like to them, that they whom he had been with before had recanted, and should not therefore suffer death, counselling them to do the like. But they answered as their brethren had done, that their faith was not builded on man, but on Christ and His Word. Now when he saw it booted not to persuade (for they were, God be praised, surely grounded on the Rock Jesus Christ), he led them to the place where they should suffer; and being all there together, most earnestly they prayed unto God, and joyfully went to the stake, and kissed it, and embraced it very heartily. The eleven men were tied to the three stakes, and the two women loose in the midst without any stake, and so they were all burnt in one fire, with such love to each other, and constancy in our Saviour Christ, that it made all the lookers-on to marvel."

The Quakers came in for persecution from all sides. Here is an example of what happened when a Quaker did not pay the tithe (one-tenth) due to the Church of England:

In 1657, Elizabeth Maynard, a poor widow, for tithe of about 2s., had now taken from her by distress. Also Richard North, of Yardley, for in tithe of an acre of wheat, valued at £5, had his house ransacked by a bayliff when only two little children

*were at home; he took away, besides all household goods, the
wearing apparel of the man himself and his children, and the
covering of their beds, for want of which they were each
prejudiced in their health, the weather being cold.* [Joseph
Besse, Sufferings of the Quakers]

England did not have to endure the bloody reign of Mary for
long. In 1558, just five years after her reign had begun, Mary died,
and Elizabeth ascended to the throne. She soon restored the
Church of England to its position as the established church.

Queen Mary, 1553-58.

Queen Elizabeth, 1558-1603

If your ancestors were devout Catholic in the latter part of the
sixteenth century, there was no way they could have open meetings
and worship in the Catholic form. They were supposed to attend
the Church of England, which many of them did. Some of them
had their children christened there and were married there themselves, but if the opportunity arose to have a traveling papist priest
"redo" these ceremonies, it was taken.

These traveling priests traveled secretly, many of them even
living with the wealthier Catholics in their large homes. Private
chapels were built so that the family and the servants could hold
Mass on Sunday.

Here is an example of a priest hiding in his secret hiding place in
one of these large homes for two days whilst the house was being
searched:

*Between Thaxted and Saffron Walden, Essex, is Broadoaks.
Today it is a farm, but in the sixteenth century it was a
magnificent place, where its owners, the Wisemans, lived in*

splendor. Most of the mansion was pulled down long ago, but the most interesting part has, fortunately, been preserved and can be seen by the public.

The Wisemans were devoted Catholics and recusants, much persecuted for their faith. During one of the many raids on Broadoaks were found not only arms, a suit of armor, bows and arrows, but also an old priest, Thomas Jackson, together with everything necessary to celebrate Mass, hidden between two walls.

Disregarding the danger involved, another priest, Father John Gerard, went there to live. Careful preparations had been made. All Protestant servants were replaced by Catholics, and an architect, Nicholas Owen, added new hiding places. He probably worked by night, putting up an elaborate fireplace in the living room during the day to account for his presence.

The chapel was at the top of the house, with only one door from a dark stair. But a small window could be used to reach the roof; and a trapdoor in the ceiling, to reach the attics. These were useful to lead the raiders away from what was concealed under their very noses. Owen made a false hearth in the chapel and burrowed underneath into solid brickwork. The gained space, situated high up, adjoined the living room, separated from it only by lath and plaster with a paneled wainscot.

The hiding place was two feet wide, and nowhere was it higher than six feet five inches. Father Gerard was a very tall man. He could stretch his legs only by sitting on two brick steps left at the bottom of the hole, but could not lie down.

Careful as all concerned had been, they made a big mistake. John Frank, a former Protestant servant, had retired to London; but the family still trusted him, and he came frequently to Broadoaks bringing messages and letters and giving a hand with urgent work, while being all the time an informer for the authorities.

Just before Easter 1594, Father Gerard went to London. Frank told the pursuivants of the opportunity. Gerard's lodgings were raided, but he was out and spent the night with his superior, Father Garnet. Father Gerard's servant, thought to be a priest, was arrested. The authorities summoned Wiseman. When he arrived in London he too was promptly arrested and put into the Tower. Frank was permitted to visit him, and Wiseman, unwittingly, revealed Father Gerard's whereabouts.

The priest had by this time returned to Broadoaks to make preparations for the Easter services. Frank was sent to

Broadoaks with two letters, one for Father Gerard from his servant and one for Mrs. Wiseman. Selected pursuivants and soldiers followed Frank, and local magistrates surrounded the house while Gerard and Mrs. Wiseman were reading their letters in Frank's presence.

Suddenly a great noise was heard, and Gerard hurried off to his hiding place. Frank rushed down to the entrance and put up a show of resisting the invaders.

There were no provisions in the hiding place, and in the upheaval Mrs. Wiseman could find only two biscuits and some quince jelly.

Father Gerard heard his enemies stamping and shouting all over the house. They did not find him but locked up Mrs. Wiseman, her two daughters, and the Catholic servants in one of the rooms. The raiders then broke down parts of the walls which sounded hollow. Knowing the priest to be in the house, they carried on for two days. Poor Father Gerard, without food and unable to sleep, could hear the mob talking and feared to ʰe discovered at any moment.

Frank continued to act the friend of the family. He was left in charge of the place when the raiders said that Mrs. Wiseman and the Catholic servants were to be taken to London. Frank promised to call the priest's name from the living room. Instead he revealed all Mrs. Wiseman had told him to the magistrates, who started another search, again without result. Infuriated, they pulled all panels and plaster off the walls.

Faggots were kept in the false fireplace, and at night they were set alight to warm the raiders. Gerard had to crouch in the back of the hole to escape the hot embers. Soon the guards discovered that the bottom of the hearth was only wood, but did nothing about it because they were called to do some more searching in other parts of the house. They kept on devastating the place but did not find the priest. In the end, thinking he must have escaped, they went away.

The inhabitants barricaded the door and rescued Father Gerard, who by now was in a terrible condition from lack of food and sleep.

****

Broadoaks experienced many more raids. Through Frank's treachery, Gerard and Nicholas Owen were later arrested at the Countess of Arundel's house. Friends bought Owen's release, and Gerard escaped from the Tower. Wiseman was caught again and found in possession of a rosary and forbidden books. He was soon released and lived to be knighted by James I, not for his merits but for a fee.

The last member of this branch of the Wiseman family was

killed in a duel in 1678.

****

Most of Broadoaks has suffered much from alterations and time. The chapel is still in good condition. Father Gerard's hiding place can be examined. No signs could be found of how fresh air entered the place. Several false fireplaces, panels, and doors have been found. At the top of the main staircase is a big trapdoor by which the upper part of the house could be completely shut off. In the garden there is still a very old quince tree, and from its fruit Mrs. Wiseman may have made the jelly she gave to Gerard.

****

There are secret hiding places in several stately homes in Essex, particularly around Thaxted.

Northend, near Dunmow, belonged to Mrs. Wiseman's mother. For many years she was persecuted, and once was nearly tortured to death.

Not far away is Leighs or Leez Priory, once the home of Lady Penelope Rich, who was converted by old Mrs. Wiseman.

At White Notley Hall, near Witham, a well-preserved refuge can be seen.

The main refuge for priests was Ingatestone Hall, between Brentwood and Chelmsford. It is said that the hiding place there is still unspoiled. [Adapted from Julia Hurst, ***Essex Countryside***.]

PRIEST HOLE,
PARHAM HALL, SUSSEX.

Another very important thing in the lives of our ancestors through the centuries, besides the church, was the local fair. Fairs can be traced back to at least Norman times, and they continued through all the centuries dealt with in this book. A charter for such privileges as holding markets and fairs had to be granted by the king.

Fairs were held in all the large towns at least once each year. To the fair came the merchants with their goods. Booths were set up in a designated open area adjoining the town. The church bells announced the opening of the fair. There were minstrel shows, ale tasting and many things reminiscent of our fairs today.

Fairs lasted for several days. For those caught stealing, "court of piepowder" was held on the spot. A man could be hanged at once after a trial by this hastily convened court. Those attending the fair would often see a man hanged on the gallows outside the fair, a reminder to keep their fingers clean.

Markets were held more frequently in the towns or boroughs than were fairs, sometimes once a week or even twice. On market day farmers from outlying parishes would bring in their crops for sale. The market was wholly devoted to the buying and selling of goods and was a popular crossroads for all segments of society.

The cattle market was very important to the farmer, as were the stalls from which he sold his field produce. Yes, market day was and still is a very important day in the lives of the English.

If your ancestors lived in a market town, all kinds of things, exciting to the children no doubt, could happen on market day. If they lived on Sheep Street in Banbury, Oxfordshire, they, like the other householders, probably set out a sheep pen and charged the farmers for its use--enterprising ancestors and an appropriate name for the street.

Fish is an important part of the Englishman's diet, but in the sixteenth century it had to be sold close to the harbor in which the catch was landed because there was no way of keeping it fresh in large quantities. As transportation improved, however, no place became very far from the sea, and fish has been eaten in abundance ever since.

Everyone knows that a fisherman's life was rough, hardy, and dangerous. It is comparatively easy to get background on your fishermen ancestors, so many stories have been written about them.

Like other things, methods of keeping law and order were changing in the sixteenth century. Whereas the lord of the manor had handled such matters on his estate, justices of the peace were now administering justice. They helped maintain law and order within the county and passed judgment on local problems. In this early example (1592) they are assessing rates of wages:

Taylors' and Shoomakers' Servants

A taylor servant of the best sorte with meate and drinke and
  without a leverye shall not take more by the year then liijs.
  (53 shillings)

A taylor of the seconde sorte as aforesaid not more by the years
  then   xljs.
  (41 shillings)

A taylor of the worste sorte as aforesayd not more by the yeare
  then   xxxs.
  (30 shillings)

A shoomaker servant of the best sorte beinge married to have
  withowte meate and drinke for ever dosin of shooes xxijd.
  (22 shillings)

A shomaker servant of the beste sorte beinge unmarried to
  have by the yeare with meate and drinke and withowte
  a leverye   liijs. iiijd.
  (54 shillings, 4 pence)

A shomaker servant of the second sorte being unmarried to have by the yeare with meate and drinke and withowte a leverye   *xlvis. viijd.*
(46 shillings, 8 pence)

A shomaker servant of the third sorte beinge unmarried to have by the yeare with meate and drinke and withowte a leverye   *xlis.*
(41 shillings)

The rates rated the last yeare to stande withowte alteration.
[***Hertford County Records,*** vol. I, p. 12]

Close by to the parish church, often on the village green, was erected the pillory, or stocks, for wrongdoers. The one being punished sat with his legs locked in the stocks and was subject to the jeers and taunts and rotten eggs of passersby.

The ducking stool, another device for wrongdoers, was a rude chair fixed on the end of a long pole that could swivel on several upright supports. The punishment, being ducked several times in the village pond, was usually reserved for women or suspected witches.

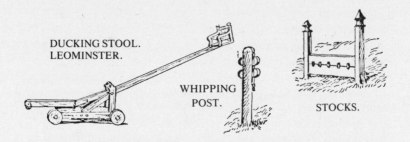

DUCKING STOOL.
LEOMINSTER.

WHIPPING
POST.

STOCKS.

Nowadays, criminals occasionally break out of jail. Apparently our ancestors occasionally broke out of the stocks, as related in this incident from the Heybridge, Essex, quarter sessions rolls for 1577, recorded in A. C. Edwards's *English History from Essex Sources: 1550-1750* (Chelmsford: County Council of Essex, 1952), p. 39:

We [the High Constables] *find that two rogues, a man and a woman, were sent by warrant by master Appeltone from constable to constable being brought to the constables of Heybridge and they setting them into the stocks fast locked and each of them a lock of their feet, and they breaking out of the stocks in the night and went their ways and the aforesaid constables made hue and cry after them with speed and could not find them.*

The stocks and whipping post at Bottesford, Leics., now very much decayed.

The Statute of Winchester of 1285 required all men with £10 in lands or 20 marks in goods to keep a complete set of armor. Those with £15 in lands or 40 marks in goods were also to keep a horse. Thus, in the absence of a standing army, troops of a sort were available for the national defense. At periodic musters, local officials were required to inspect the equipment and issue a certificate. Records were kept of these musters or surveys, and some have been preserved.

In the military survey for the town of Exeter for 1522 there appear several interesting items (the lists cover not only males over 16 years of age but a few female landowners also): ". . . *William Peryman, a bow, a half sheaf of arrows.*" Many listed as bowmen had only half a sheaf of arrows; other had just a bow; and others just had the protective harness.

Some of those listed as billmen had no bills, some had swords, some just harness. Among the lists of those ''not able for war'' are many who have considerable equipment. Perhaps their unfitness was a result of previous involvement:

Early Tudor Musketeer and Pikeman.

John Germyn, a pair of brigandines [body armor], *a sallet* [helmet] *2 bills, and a pole axe*

Andrew Mannyng, a pair of splints, anabow, 2 sheaves of arrows, a bill, a fall of mail and a pair of gussets [Adapted from **Tudor Exeter,** Devon and Cornwall Record Society, New Series, vol. 22]

A splint was a small plate of metal in the armor; a gusset was a piece of chain mail at the openings of the joints of the plate armor.

ARMY ON THE MARCH

The wars and religious turmoil of the sixteenth century almost certainly touched the lives of your ancestors in some way. But for most of your ancestors, life followed the familiar cycles of birth, marriage, and death, with the intervening periods generally ruled by routine. This is not to say that your ancestors were not interesting. The records we have of them often reveal rich insights into their singular personalitites. A veritable biographical goldmine is this type of burial entry, which occasionally occurs in parish registers in any century. The method of recording was, of course, entirely dependent on the nature of the parish minister:

Margerie Deconsonne the wife of Bartholomew Deconsonne. . . fiftie yeares of age a tall slender woman, providently thrifty, perhaps I should say rather stingy shee leaving this life on Monday was buried on Tuesday the 30 of Aprill (1588) [From W. E. Tate, *The Parish Chest* (Cambridge, 1951)]

If your ancestor was fortunate enough to go to school--and very few were--this is how a normal school day went (Winchester, about 1550):

5:00 a.m.	Get up, dress, wash, and make the bed
5:30 a.m.	To the chapel for a religious service
6:00 to 9:00 a.m.	Lessons
9:00 a.m.	Breakfast
9:30 to 12:00 noon	Lessons
12:00 noon	Dinner

1:00 to 3:30 p.m.	Lessons
3:30 p.m.	Beer
4:00 to 5:00 p.m.	Lessons
5:00 p.m.	Prayers and relaxation
6:00 p.m.	Evening meal
6:30 to 7:45 p.m.	Homework
7:45 p.m.	Supper
8:00 p.m.	To the chapel to sing a psalm
8:15 p.m.	Off to bed

Studies were confined to grammar, logic, arithmetic, Latin, and Greek.

Just as it does today, tragedy struck in many families, disturbing the comfortable routines of daily life. The following was contributed by E. M. Gooday to the *Sussex Family History* magazine.

The entries in the East Dean register for the year 1559/1560 include this burial of two sisters on the same day:

"Agnes Payne the daughter of Edward Payne was buryed the first day of february.

"Johan Payne the daughter of Edward Payne was buryed the first day of february."

When, in 1598, Arthur Pollard, then vicar of East Dean, came to these entries as he was making the present copy of the original register, he added the following interesting story:

"In ye death of these two sisters last mentioned is one thinge worthy recordinge diligently to be noted. The elder sister called Agnes being very sicke unto ye deathe speachles and was thought past hope of speakinge after she had lyen 24 houres without speach at last upon a suddayne cryed out to her sister to make herselfe ready and to come with her: her sister Johan being abroad about other business was called for who being come to her sick sister demaunding how she did. She very lowde and earnestly bad her sister make her ready. She stayed for her and could not go without her: within halfe an houre after Johan was taken very sicke which increasinge all night uppon her, her other sister still calling her to come away, in the morning they both departed this wretched world together. O the unsearchable wisdome of god how depe are his judgments and his ways past fyndinge out.

"Testified by divers ould and honest persons yet livinge which I my selfe have hard their father whilst he was alive report.

Arth. Pollard vicar"

If your ancestor was, by profession a customs or excise officer, his task was often quite dangerous. The smuggling of taxable goods was common and difficult to keep in check. The diary of one Henry Machyn illustrates this:

Sailors arresting smugglers.

The Xiij day of Marche [1551] *was hangyd at Smythfield* [London] *one John Mosbe and ys syster, for the death of a gentylman of Fayversham, one M. Arden, the Customer and ys owne wyff was decaul . . . .* [hanged?] *and she was burnyd at Canterbury* [Kent] *and her servant hangyd there, and ij at Feyversham and one at Hospryng, and anodur in he way to Canterbury, for the death of M. Arden of Feyversham. And at Flushing* [Kent] *was burnyd Blake Tome* [Black Tom] *for the sam deth of M. Arden.* [From Edward Carson, *The Ancient and Rightful Customs* (Lond: Faber & Faber, 1972)

Summary justice!

Your ancestors had little opportunity for recreation. They were officially restricted from playing many games and sports. This is true not only in the sixteenth century, but in later centuries also.

An act passed in 1541 lists different groups by trade who were so restricted. They included most males. The intent was possibly to force the men to become skilled in archery, the only sport not banned, in order to provide a group of trained men who could be called upon in a military emergency. Many of your ancestors are bound to have broken such a severe law.

Cards and dice were the most common games. They must have developed into a widespread and serious problem because there are hundreds of examples of people being punished for playing these games. The local constables were kept busy. Even schoolmasters were indicted. And in 1590 one parish minister because so absorbed in his gambling habits that he neglected to conduct Divine Service.

10 of May the Boorke of Sportes upon the Lords day was burnt by the Hangman in the place where the Croffe Itoode. & at Exhange

THE BURNING OF THE BOOK OF SPORTS,
From an engraving by W. Hollar 1643

All the wealthy families employed gardeners and maintained beautiful flower gardens. Often the flower beds were edged with rosemary, lavender, marjoram, and thyme. Red currants and black currants were introduced from the Continent.

It is likely that the working class in the countryside maintained flower gardens too, depending on the space available and the need to grow their own food. Many of your ancestors are described as gardeners on the landowners' estates.

Musical instuments had developed from single strings and horns. The viol was played like a violin; the viola da gamba was a similar instrument, played between the knees. The lute looked like a modern mandolin.

A Lady Playing a Virginal.

ITALIAN SPINET GIVEN BY THE
QUEEN OF SAXONY TO QUEEN ELIZABETH

The spinet had developed from the harp. The piano is the outcome of the dulcimer and the spinet. The organ had been in use for a long time.

The clarion was a trumpet; the shawm and pomme, whistle flutes. The hornpipe was exactly that--a horn at the end of a long pipe.[1]

---

[1]The paragraphs on gardens and musical instruments were adapted from Marjorie and C.H.B. Quennell, *A History of Everyday Things in England,* rev. ed. (London: Batsford, 1960).

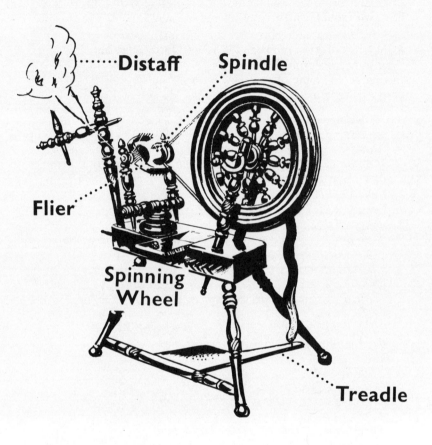

Distaff   **Spindle**

Flier

Spinning Wheel

Treadle

The old fashioned spinning wheel, object of thousands of hours of our ancestors' time. Every home had at least one.

Although this book deals mostly with working-class living, an occasional glimpse of how the wealthy lived provides interesting comparisons. As the royal head and his retinue traveled from place to place throughout the realm, they stayed overnight in the homes of knights or nobles. Sometimes this was an embarrassment to the host, who could ill afford the high cost of such a visit.

From the account books of Sir William Petre of Ingatestone Hall, Essex, in 1561 (now in the Essex Record Office and printed in *English History from Essex Sources: 1550-1750,* pp. 27-28), comes this record of some of the food provided for a three-day visit by Queen Elizabeth.

A declaration of all such provision of victuals and other necessaries as was bought and provided against the Queen's Majesty's coming to my master's house at Ingatestone, being the 19th day of July in the third year of her Majesty's reign, and there tarrying until the 22nd of the same, both days included, viz.

2½ qrs. white wheat at 22s. the qr., 55s.

4 doz. of bread bought, 4s.

2 tun of beer and ale at 33s. 4d. the tun, with 6s. 8d. carriage, £ 3 13s. 4d.

4 barrels of beer at 5d. the barrel

Certain sea fish, viz., soles, flounders, gurnards, congers and other sea fish, besides certain sea fish given to my master, £ 3 4s.

2 firkins of sturgeon at 23s. 4d. the piece, 46s. 8d.

6 cygnets at 10. the piece, 60s.

6 doz. pewits, whereof 2 doz. at 18s. the doz., the rest at 16s the doz., £ 5

One doz. gulls at 3s 4d. the piece, 40s.

2 doz brewes at 2s. the piece, 48s.

2 doz egrets at 2s. the piece, 48s.

The carriage of said fowl from London, 6s. 8d.

12 herons and 12 shovellers bought at London at 2s. 6d. the piece, £ 3

18 herons at 22d. the piece, bought in Kent, 33s.

12 shovellers at 12d. the piece, bought in Kent, 12s.

12 doz. of quails at 4s. the doz., bought at London, 48s.

4 cygnets bought at Cambridge at 7s. the piece, 6d. in the whole abated, 27s. 6d.

6 bitterns bought there at 18d. the piece, with 2d. over in the whole 9s. 2d.

27 geese at 5d. the piece, 6s. 3d.

26 caponets at 16d. the piece, 34s. 8d.

14 caponets at 8d. the piece, 9s. 4d.

One doz. pullets at 4d. the piece, 4s.

4 doz. chickens at 3s. the doz., 12s.

1 doz. of chickens at 2 ½d. the piece, 2s. 6d.

6 caponets bought at London, 2 at 3s. the piece, the rest at 2s. 8d. the piece, 16s. 8d.

1 doz. caponets for 13s. 4d. and 2 doz. chickens for 7s., 20s. 4d.

693 eggs, 15s. 7d.

14 dishes of butter at 7d. the dish, 8s. 2d.

5 gallons of cream at 8d. the gallon, 3s. 4d.

Bullocks' livers to feed fowl, 16d.

Yeast and herbs for the kitchen, 18d.

Hemp seed, 4½bushels at 3s. 4d. the bushel, 1d, over, 15s. 1d.

A barrel of samphire, 12d., one barrel olives containing one gallon and a pint, 3s., one barrel of capers containing 3 lb., 7s. 8d.

200 oranges, 19¼d.

Comfits of sundry sorts, 28s. 6d.

Sugar, cloves, mace, pepper and sundry other kind of spice, ut patet per billam, £ 7 15s.

12 lb. prunes sent to my lady, 16d.

½ peck of fine white salt, 2½d.

Fruit, viz. pears, plums and genetings, 2s.

7 baskets of sundry sorts sent from London with necessary things, 3s 7s.

Mr. Apleton's man for a fresh salmon, 3s. 4d.

Young's man of Willesden, for bringing a turkey cock and ½ doz. pea chickens, 8d.

A London Water-Carrier.

THE SEVENTEENTH CENTURY

HISTORICAL	RELIGIOUS	RECORD-KEEPING	SOCIAL, ECONOMICAL
1603 JAMES THE FIRST (1603-25).		1603 Further reiteration of previous acts concerning the keeping of parish registers.	1601 A new Poor Law Act designed to reduce vagrancy was passed. Great struggles for civil and religious liberty resulted in colonization of North America.
1607 Jamestown, Virginia, founded by Captain John Smith.	1606 Groups of Separatists fled to Holland.		
	1611 King James, or Authorized Version of the Bible published.		
	1614 Some Separatists returned to London and established a church which later became known as the General Baptists.		
1618 Beginning of the Thirty Years' War with Germany.	1620 Congregationalists sailed on the Mayflower and founded Plymouth Colony in Massachusetts Bay.		
1621 New York settled by the Dutch.			
1625 CHARLES THE FIRST (1625-49).			
1626 Charles and Parliament struggled for power. War with France and Spain.			
1629 Parliament dissolved by the King. It did not meet for another eleven years.			
1642 Beginning of the Civil War. Battle of Edgehill.	1643 England and Scotland signed a covenant to bring about changes in religion and government and to extirpate popery.	1642 Commencement of the Civil Wars, during which some parish registers were ill-kept and earlier records were lost or destroyed.	
1643 Battle of Roundaway Hill and seige of Gloucester.		1644 Earliest known date in known Presbyterian registers.	
1644 Battles of Cropredy Bridge, Marston Moor, Newbury, and Tippermuir.			

THE INDEPENDENTS CLAIMING
LIBERTY OF CONSCIENCE. 1643.

THE SEVENTEENTH CENTURY

HISTORICAL	RELIGIOUS	RECORD-KEEPING	SOCIAL, ECONOMICAL
1645 Battles of Naseby and Philliphaugh.	1647 Presbyterians came to power in both church and government.	1644 Earliest date in known Independent (Congregational) registers.	
1648 Battle of Preston.	1648 The Westminster (Presbyterian) Confession of Faith.	1647 Earliest date in known Baptist registers.	1649 Great strides made toward full representation of the people.
1649 Charles I executed. The Commonwealth established and the monarchy abolished.	1649 George Fox, founder of the Society of Friends (or Quakers), commenced his preaching. First Welsh Baptist Church founded at Swansea, Glamorgan.		
1650 Battle of Dunbar, Scotland.			
1651-52 Battle of Worcester, union with Scotland, and war with Holland.	1653 The meetings of the various Nonconformist groups began to increase in number	1653 Provincial probate courts abolished and all probates granted in London only (1653-60).	
1653 OLIVER CROMWELL became lord protector.		1653 Justices of the peace alone empowered to solemnize marriages. The parish clerk to record births, marriages, and deaths. Some parish registers not kept at all. This condition lasted until 1660.	
1654 War with Spain, which left England mistress of the seas. Capture of Jamaica.	1657 A few Jews were permitted to settle in England.		
1658 Battle of the Dunes. Capture of Dunkirk. Death of Oliver Cromwell.	1660 The ejected ministers returned to their livings.	1654-61 Many Quaker records commenced about this time.	
1658-60 RICHARD CROMWELL (son of Oliver) lord protector.		1660 Provincial probate courts reopened.	
1660 CHARLES THE SECOND (1660-85).			

CROMWELL LEAVING THE HOUSE OF COMMONS, 1649.

HISTORICAL	RELIGIOUS	RECORD-KEEPING	SOCIAL, ECONOMICAL
1662 Act of Uniformity.	1662 About 2,000 vicars and rectors were driven from their parishes for being Nonconformists (Presbyterians and Independents). Persecution of all Nonconformists. Presbyterianism disestablished. Episcopalian Church of England restored. New system of Poor Law administration lasted until 1834.	1663 Earliest date in known Roman Catholic registers.	1665 The great plague of London.
1665 War with Holland.	1671-72 Declaration of Indulgence freed Nonconformists from prison and permitted their free worship.	1667 Burials in woolen enforced by law to help support the declining wool trade.	1666 The great fire of London.
1672 War with Holland. British army increased to 10,000 men.	1672 The Test Act excluded Roman Catholics from public office.	1669 Earliest date in known German Lutheran registers.	
1679 The Habeas Corpus Act was passed.		1679 Burials in woolen more strictly enforced.	
1682 Pennsylvania founded by William Penn.		1684 Huguenot French Protestant registers commence in London.	
1685 JAMES THE SECOND (1685-89, died 1701).			

HISTORICAL	RELIGIOUS	RECORD-KEEPING	SOCIAL, ECONOMICAL
1685 Monmouth rebellion and battle of Sedgemoor. British army raised to 20,000 men.	1685 Revocation of the Edict of Nantes drove thousands of Protestants (Huguenots) out of France, many of whom settled in England.		
1688 Army raised to 40,000. William of Orange landed in England.			1688 Bill of Rights
1689 WILLIAM (1689-1702) and MARY (died 1694). Siege of Londonderry.	1689 The Presbyterian Church established by law in Scotland. The Toleration Act permitted freedom of worship for Protestant Nonconformists. Bill of Rights passed.	1689 Earliest known Royal Dutch Chapel registers commence.	
1690 Battle of the Boyne. 1692 French intention to invade England came to naught.	1695 Act of Parliament imposed a fine upon all who failed to inform the parish minister of the birth of a child. This act repealed in 1706.	1695 Commencement of lists in parish registers of "dissenters," children born but not christened in the parish church. Some were called *papist* and others *recusants* 1698 Duties (taxes) imposed on entries in parish registers. Repealed after five years.	1693- Bank of England 94 established. Board of Trade formed.

HOME-THOUGHTS, FROM ABROAD

O to be in England now that April's there
And whoever wakes in England sees, some morning,
*   unaware,*
That the lowest boughs and the brushwood sheaf
Round the elm-tree bole are in tiny leaf,
While the chaffinch sings on the orchard bough
In England--now!

And after April, when May follows,
And the whitethroat builds, and all the swallows!
Hark, where my blossom'd pear-tree in the hedge
Leans to the field and scatters on the clover
Blossoms and dewdrops--at the bent spray's edge--
That's the wise thrush; he sings each song twice
*   over,*
Lest you should think he never could recapture
The first fine careless rapture!
And though the fields look rough with hoary dew,
All will be gay when noontide wakes anew
The buttercups, the little children's dower
--Far brighter than this gaudy melon-flower!

*   -Robert Browning (1812-1899)*

Chapter Two

THE SEVENTEENTH CENTURY

All tennants of an ancient place
And heirs of noble heritage
Coeval they with Adams race
And blest with more substantial age
For when the world first saw the sun
These little flowers beheld him too
And when his love for earth begun
They were the first his smiles to woo . . .

Time looks on pomp with careless moods
Or killing apathys disdain
--So where old marble citys stood
Poor persecuted weeds remain
She feels a love for little things
That very few can feel beside
And still the grass eternal springs
Where castles stood and grandeur died

From Clares, "The Flitting"

As the seventeenth century dawned, Elizabeth I still occupied the throne of England. During her lengthy reign, the longest by a British sovereign in over two centuries, she had brought badly needed stability to the lives of our ancestors. Under her able administration, England prospered, and many people were free to go about their lives relatively undisturbed.

For your laborer ancestors, life in the 1600s follows a familiar pattern. From March to September, work in the fields went on from 5:00 a.m. to 7:30 p.m. Half an hour was allowed for breakfast, and hour for dinner, and an hour for "drinkings." On hot summer days a half hour was allowed for a nap.

In winter work went on from sun up to sun down.

A careful watch was kept for workers who tried to organize other groups of workers into combinations. Those who did were severely punished. It wasn't until the nineteenth century that trade unions began to establish themselves.

In the 1600s many of our present huge industrial centers were merely small country villages.

This period saw large migrations of Huguenots come into England from France, particularly after 1685. Between 1670 and

1690 about 80,000 came to England.
They settled in the towns, princi-
pally London, and soon benefited
the English silk trade, the sailcloth
trade, and the hatmaking and
papermaking trades by their skills.

WINDING SILK.
(From an old print.)

Throughout the centuries, various methods were used to obtain
revenue to finance the country. The one shown below, for the year
1621, shows those who paid taxes in certain Northamptonshire
parishes.

Because the number is small, obviously this tax was affecting the
more well to do in the parish.

SUBSIDY, 1621

PASSENAM AND DENSHANGER.

Mr. Richard Pledwell
   goodes.................... *vli.—*   *viijs.*   *iiijd.*
Mr. William Carpentar la........ *iijli.—*   *xijs.*
William Thorne la:............. *xxs.—*   *iiijs.*
George Thorne ges............ *iijli.—*   *viijs.*
Allexander Trutton la:......... *xxs.—*   *iijs.*
Robert Clarke ges............. *iijli.—*   *viijs.*   *ijli. viijs, iiijd.*

PAULERSPERRY AND HETHENCOTT

Sir Arthur Throckmorton
   knight la:.................. *xxli.—*   *iijli.*
Thomas Boughton ges.......... *iijli.—*   *viijs.*
Thomas Cardell ges............ *iijli.—*   *viijs.*
Roger Peake ges.............. *iijli.—*   *viijs.*
John Bussher la:.............. *xls.—*   *viijs.*
Richard Webbe ges............ *iijli.—*   *viijs.*
John Haille la:................ *xxs.—*   *iiijs.*   *vjli. iiijs.*

[*fo.* 320] YARDLEY GOBION

Thomas Smith alias
   Kent goodes................ *iijli.—*   *viijs.*
John Browne ges.............. *iijli.—*   *viijs.*
William Smith alias
   Caues ges.................. *iijli.—*   *viijs.*
Thomas Scotte ges............ *iijli.—*   *viijs.*
William Warrington ges........ *iijli.—*   *viijs.*
Peter Boughton la............. *xls.—*   *viijs.*
Thomas Smith alias
   Caues la................... *xls.—*   *viijs.*
John Goodman la:............. *xxs.—*   *iiijs.*   *iijli.*

ASHTON

Sir Robart Osborne la.......... *xxli.—*   *iiij li.*
Anthony Maryatt ges.......... *vli.—*   *xiijs.*   *iiijd.*
John Marryatt ges............. *iiijli. —*   *xs.*   *viijd.*
[William Harryson]
   [John Wright] ges .... *iijli.—*   *vs.*   *viijd.*

John Marryat of the
Spoute ges.................. *iijli.* —   *viijs.*   *vjli [vjs.ᵈ]*

Many young men were apprenticed to skilled craftsmen in order for them to learn trades. Instructions to apprentices vary only slightly from area to area and from century to century. Here is one example:

INSTRUCTIONS FOR THE APPRENTICES.

YOU should constantly and devoutly, every Morning and Evening, in the most humble Manner, worship God, and say your Prayers. And when you shall have your Master's Leave, you shall go to the public Prayers of the Church, and there behave yourself devoutly and decently. You shall carefully attend to the Sermons on the Lord's Day, and endeavour to fix them upon your Mind, and be sure to practise them in your Life and Conversation. You shall reverence and obey all your Superiors and Governors. You shall do diligent and faithful Service to your Master for the Time of your Apprentice-ship; and deal truly in what you shall be trusted. You should often read over the Covenants of your Indenture, and see and endeavour yourself to perform the same to the utmost of your Power. You should avoid evil Company, and all Occasions that may draw you thereunto; and make speedy Return when you shall be sent on your Master's or Mistress's Errands. You should avoid Idleness, and be ever employed either in God's Service, or in your Master's Business. You should be of fair, gentle and lowly Speech and Behaviour to all Men; and according to your Deserts expect your Reward for Good or Ill from God and your Friends. But, for your better Help and Instruction to the Performance of your Duty, you will do well often to read, and seriously to consider, the Holy Scriptures, so in particular those Passages therein which direct Servants how to behave themselves; some few whereof are here inserted, and recommended to your frequent Perusal and Practice: EPHESIANS, Chap. vi. Ver. 5, 6, 7, 8. COLOSSIANS, Chap. iii. Ver. 22, 23, 24, 25. The first Epistle to TIMOTHY, Chap. vi. Ver. 1, 2. TITUS, Chap. ii. Ver 9, 10. The first Epistle of PETER, Chap. ii. Ver. 18, 19, 20. Many more your own Diligence may supply. So God direct you and assist you in the Performance of your Duty.

GOD SAVE THE QUEEN.

A London apprentice talking with two housewives.

Besides the apprentice, whose parents could afford to pay a premium to have him learn a trade, there were the poor apprentices, farmed out from the parishes and boroughs. No premiums were paid for them. In most cases the parishes were glad to get rid of the obligation to feed and clothe these youth, who were often the children of unwed mothers or widows or who were orphans. Doubtless there were some poor apprentices who lived at home and whose parents allowed them to go off to an apprenticehsip. Often these poor apprentices turned out to be merely servants without pay, except for board, food, and clothing-- and even that of the bare minimum. So when we read such stories as the one that follows, we need to keep this background in mind. The story appears in the Essex quarter sessions and is printed in *English History from Essex Sources: 1550-1750,* pages 46 and 47.

The most humble petition of William Noone of Billericay, barber and painter.

That whereas (almost four years since) the parishioners of Hutton did put an apprentice unto me called Stephen Thorpe, then aged between 9 and 10 years, whom your petitioner hath carefully maintained with meat, drink, apparel and all other things sufficient and necessary for such a servant, tendering him as my own child, and not anywise abusing him with hard usage or unreasonable correction, as shall and will be testified by the parishioners of Billericay my neighbours who have hereunto subscribed. But may it please your Honours and Worships to be advertised that the said Stephen Thorpe, my apprentice, is (though young in years) of a most wicked and thievish disposition, and hath done many and sundry robberies, and broken above twenty walls; for which he hath been thrice in the House of Correction (where he now remaineth) and once in the Gaol at Colchester (from whence he was delivered but the last Michaelmas Quarter Sessions). But wickedness is so rooted in him that there is no hope of amendment, for that he groweth from evil to worse, and threateneth to do more mischief than ever he hath done. And forsomuch as by means of the said wicked boy your poor orator is utterly undone for ever, my humble petition to this honourable court is that I may be quite released of the said boy . . .

We the inhabitants of Great Burstead and Billericay whose names are hereunto subscribed, do hereby testify the said William Noone to be an honest man and of good behaviour; and that the former petition is true in every particular. And we likewise humbly request that the poor man may (by this honourable court) be released of the said naughty boy.

[16 signatures]

Your working-class ancestors in the seventeenth century really knew what inflation meant. While wages rose 200 percent, the cost of living rose 600 percent. Wages simply rose at the whim of the employer. Where a worker in the previous century could earn a certain amount in seventeen weeks, it now took a whole year to earn the same amount. With such a tremendous rate of inflation, it is no wonder that many people could not earn enough to support themselves.

At the bottom of the social strata were the laborers. Under the old manorial system, the laborer could pay rent to the lord of the manor by working on the lord's land. But land enclosure, which favored raising sheep to everyday foodstuffs, still continued in this century and required less labor. Many families were thrown off their manorial strips of land and had to hire themselves out where they could. These ancestors became known as *vagabonds* and *vagrants,* because they were on the move almost continually. The two words did not have the negative connotations they do today.

Poor people were in abundance. Since each civil parish was always short of funds to support those people who were unable to work, serious attempts were made to determine whose responsibility it was to support the poor. Accounts of such attempts provide good insights into the living conditions of our poorer ancestors.

Vagabonds, 1609

Humphrey Beddow, a lame man, was borne in the Parish of Cardington: hee was sett apprentice in the same Parish to a shoemaker and there served his time; afterwards hee came to worke journey worke in this Parish [Middle], and marryed Mary the daughter of Thomas Davis of Haremeare Hill. Note, that att this time 40 dayes' continuance as an housekeeper, servant or sojourner without disturbance did create a settlement in any parish. Note alsoe that if the Parish officers did require any person to avoid out of the Parish or to finde suretyes, this was not accompted a disturbance. Butt a complaint made to a Justice of Peace that such a person was come into a parish and was likely to beecome chargeable to the parish-this complaint was a legall disturbance without takeing out a warrant, and the Justices' Clerks did commonly keep a booke and enter all disturbances; butt if a warrant was taken out this was a proofe of the complaint and disturbance.

After Humphry Beddow was married, a complaint was made by our parish officers to Francis Thornes, Esq., and a warrant procured which was deliverd to George Cranage, who was then constable of Newton. Humphrey Beddow was then sicke, but hee promised to returne into his owne parish as soone as hee was recovered. His sicknesse was long, and although it tooke not

away his life yet it tooke away his worke, for I never knew him worke afterward butt was an idle beggard all his life after. Humphry Beddow when hee was recovered went to Cardington, his owne parish, and was sent backe by an order into this Parish. Wee appealed to the Sessions; our Counsell was Mr. Barret, and theires was Mr. Harris of Crocketon. Wee proved that Humphry Beddow was born in Cardington Parish, and there set apprentice and served out his time which was a good settlement. They alledged that hee had procured a settlement in Myddle parish by 40 dayes' residence and longer time. Our warrant of disturbance was lost, and although wee could prove that hee was disturbed yet wee could not prove that it was within the 40 days, and therefore theire order was confirmed. This was the first contest that we had and thus wee lost it; but thanks be to God wee never lost any afterwards.
[from *Antiquities and Memoirs of Myddle* (Shropshire)]

Parish overseers of the poor, afraid of the expense to their already depleted parish funds, disliked the poor passing through their parishes.

An invaluable economic indicator of this period is the accounts of the overseers of the poor. Those of Hornchurch, Essex, indicate that Widow Siggars died, leaving children to be cared for. They show how, in 1660, the overseers sold some of her worldly goods and bought clothing for one of her children. Two years later they sold more of her goods, presumably for the support of her orphaned children. What wonderful background material this would provide for a history of her family. The accounts are recorded on page 40 of *English History from Essex Sources: 1650-1750:*

1660   £ s. d.

Sold of the goods of the widow Siggars deceased to the sum of as more particularly followeth:

1 brass ladle	0. 6
1 dozen of trenchers	0. 6
1 pair of pattens and a skillet	2.10
1 kettle and a warming pan	7. 6
1 chair and a stool	1. 4
1 pair of sheets	6. 0
1 pair of scales	1. 4
1 fire iron	0. 8
2 wooden platters	0. 6
1 kettle, a wheel and a half peck	7. 0
1 trundle-bed	3. 6
4 cheese	11. 0
1 broom hook	1. 6
1 iron pot	4. 6
Of Samuel Ballard by agreement	1.0. 0

Laid out for the widow Siggars' youngest child:

For cloth for an upper coat	0.3. 4
For making the upper coat	0.2. 0
For making a body coat	0.0 8
For making a petticoat	0.0. 4
For whale-bone and other implements	0.0. 4
For 1 pair of hose, 1 pair of shoes and a cap	0.1. 8½

1662

Sold of the goods of the widow Siggars:

14 lb. of pewter at 11d. per lb.	0.12.10
A little table, 1 form and 2 joined stools	0. 8. 0
1 pair of sheets, 1 shift, 1 pair of pillowberes,	
1 coarse towel	0.10. 0
6 napkins, 4 pairs of pillowberes, 1 cap, 1 pin cushion	0.10. 0
1 old scarf	0. 1. 6
1 old shift	0. 0. 6

In the parish registers of Stevington, Bedfordshire, is recorded a typical situation:

William Aukley and Susan his pretended wife taken as sturdy beggars November 1687 whipt according to law and sent away with a passe to Margarets in ye Isle of Thanet in ye County of Kent . . . [Recorded in Tate, *The Parish Chest*]

The eastern extremity of Kent was a considerable walking distance from Bedfordshire--approximately one hundred miles! One wonders if they made it. Whose ancestors, if any, are they? What were they doing so far away from their parish of legal settlement? Would St. Margaret's Thanet accept them back, knowing they would have to provide for their support?

Here is a record of a poor woman whose house was pulled down:

1670

Upon hearing and debating of the matter in variance in court this day between Joan Selby, a poor inhabitant of Bedworth in this county, and the churchwardens and overseers of the poor there that the said Joan is destitute of an habitation, the said churchwardens and overseers of the poor or some or one of them having lately pulled down her house, it is therefore ordered by this court that the churchwardens and overseers of the poor of Bedworth aforesaid or some or one of them do upon sight hereof provide a convenient habitation for the said Joan Selby and place her therein. [**Warwick County Records,** vol. 5, p. 134]

Hungry men will do many things to provide food or money for their families. Poaching, therefore, was quite common for several hundred years. Many varieties of game were running wild and free on the estates of gentlemen, so the temptation to steal some of the game was very great. The following example is taken from **English History from Essex Sources: 1550-1750,** pages 37 and 38:

From the record book of Sir William Holcroft, Justice of the Peace, Verderer of the Forest and Captain in the Militia, 1671. Holcroft Archives, Essex Record Office.

Thomas Gallopp, one of the underkeepers to Francis Osbaston Esq., Master Keeper of Leyton Walk, brought this day one William Sparkes, of Woodford, tailor before me, whom he apprehended the day before not far from the Green Man at Leytonstone near to which place there lay a hind dead, the said Sparkes having about him a gun which was screwed off into three pieces, by which means he carried it undescried under a coat, which gun was then charged only

with powder ready to put a bullet into. Upon examination the said Sparkes confessed that he was walking from Woodford to Leytonstone with a gun intending to shoot some rabbits. Upon this confession Sir William Hicks and I committed him to the (Forest) prison at Stratford.

Whereas the principal internal conflict of the previous century had been religious--Catholics versus Protestants--the principal conflict of the seventeenth century was

VISITING PRISONERS

political. Charles I, who had come to the throne in 1625, quarreled with Parliament and finally dissolved that body. As a result, in 1642 civil war broke out between the supporters of the king, who were called Royalists or Cavaliers, and the supporters of Parliament, or the Roundheads (so called because of their short-cropped hair), who were led by Oliver Cromwell. The Roundheads were victorious, and King Charles' attempt to rule without Parliament ended in Cromwell's ruling without King Charles.

Cromwell, a Puritan, soon replaced many of the parish priests who leaned towards Catholicism.

In the events of the Civil War, which lasted from 1642 to 1649, many of your ancestors took part. In the absence of newspapers, the events of this period have to be drawn from a variety of sources. This example taken from *More Examples of English Handwriting* (Essex Record Office), shows what went on in many parts of the country:

DEPOSITIONS TAKEN BY JUSTICES
OF THE PEACE
1645

The Informacion of Robert White of the parish of Barking yeoman taken vpon oath the 28th day of June **1645** before Sr Henry Mildmay K.^{tt,} and William Toppesfeilde Esq.^s two of his Maties Justices of the peace for the said County.

The Inform^t sth, that two Monethes since or thereabouts going along Fishers streete in the towne of Barking vpon his occasions, Margaret the wife of Thomas Edwards of the same Fisherman in a violent and outragious manner called him roundheaded rogue, and said. It was long of such roundheaded rogues as hee was, that they were brought into such a condicion, vsing many other reviling words whereby a great tumult was raised in the said towne, insomuch that this Inform.^t was constrained to take a Marsh forke from a Marshman to defend himselfe from hurt and violence, wch was like to bee offered to this Inform.^t by reason of the said vproare and tumult./

The Informacion of Edmund Palmer of Barking Draper taken vpon oath vt supra./

The Inform.^tsth, that two Monethes since or thereabouts hee being then Constable, and going to demaund of Thomas Edwards of Barking Fisherman some money due vpon a rate, Margaret the wife of the said Edwards said to this Inform^t (videlicet), That a Company of yo^u had brought a Popish Preist to towne, but (s^{tn} shee) the King is a comming now, and then wee shall haue a course taken wth yo^u and such as yo^u are; or words to the like effect./

The Informacion of Nicholas Cleere of Barking Mealeman taken vpon oath vt supra./

Who sth, that this day sennight, going out of the Markett, hee heard Margarett the wife of the said Thomas Edwards say, That Mr Peter Witham Preacher of Barking placed there by the Parliam^t w.th the approbacion of the Assembly of Divines, was a Papist Dogg, And further said, That if shee had bin there (meaing att the buryall of one Margarett spence) shee would have holpe to haue torne him in peices like a Papist dogg as he was./

W^m. Toppesfeilde

A pikeman, the type of soldier forming the main body of infantry 1642-49.

TYPES OF CAVALIER SOLDIERS

ROUNDHEAD SOLDIERS.

The next example, from the same source, shows some of the results of the Civil War fighting. These entries are taken from the parish constable's accounts of the parish of Woodford, Essex, showing assistance given to poor travelers passing through or dying there and to soldiers involved in the Civil War:

Certayne moneys disbursed by Nickolas Coates and Robert Smith Constables of the parish of Wood ford in the County of Essex in Anno 1649 and part in Anno 1650 as Followeth

	l's	s	d
October 20 passed away 5 lame Cripples Charges for bread beare and horse to carry them away	0	4	6
October 28 passed away 7 poore men women Charges	0	2	8
October 31[1] passed away one lame man Charges	0	2	0
Nouember 7 passed away Three Irish women	0	1	6

Nouember 11 Quartered by Nickolas Coates and Robert
Smith 7 lame soldyers by the Comand of my lord Generall . . . . 0 . 7 . 10
Nouember 15 passed away 5 poore men Two of those men
had but one Arme a peece Charges . . . . 0 . 3 . 4

Nouember 23 passed away 13 men women and Chil
deren Charges for horse and Cart . . . . 0 . 5 . 0

While some of our ancestors lived in parts of England barely affected by the Civil War, others were right in the middle of momentous events. One interesting event, occurring in 1642, follows:

Nathaniell, the son of John Owen of Myddle, the father was hang'd before the warrs, and the son deserved it in the warrs, for hee was a Cataline to his owne country. His common practice was to come by night with a party of horse to some neighbour's house and breake open the doores, take what they pleased, and if the man of the house was found, they carryed him to prison, from whence he could not bee released without a Ransome in money; soe that noe man here about was safe from him in his bed; and many did forsoke their owne houses. This Nat. Owen was mortally wounded by some of his owne party, in a alehouse quarrell, neare Bridgenorth, and was carryed in a cart to Bridgenorth to bee healed, but in the meane time the parliament party laid seidge to Bridgenorth, and Garrison soldiers within the towne sett the towne on fire, and fledd into the Castle, in which fire, this Owen (being unable to helpe himselfe,) was burnt to death. [From *Antiquities and Memoirs of Myddle (Shropshire)*]

Cromwell died in 1658 and was followed by his son, Richard. Unfortunately, Richard was not the wise administrator his father was, and in 1660 England asked Charles II to return from France and restore the monarchy.

After the restoration of the monarchy, it was difficult for parish ministers of the Church of England to please each ruler who came to the throne. The parson's plight was satirized in a song called "The Vicar of Bray [Berkshire]":

1. In good King Charles's golden days,
   When loyalty no harm meant,
   A zealous High Churchman was I,
   And so I got preferment;
   To teach my flock I never missed,
   Kings were by God appointed,
   And lost are they that dare resist,
   Or touch the Lord's anointed.

   And this is law, that I'll maintain,
   Until my dying day, Sir,
   That whatsoever King may reign
   I'll be the Vicar of Bray, Sir.

2. When royal James possessed the crown,
   And Popery grew in fashion,
   The penal laws I hooted down,
   And read the Declaration;
   The Church of Rome I found would fit
   Full well my constitution,
   And I had been a Jesuit,
   But for the Revolution.

   And this is law, &c.

3. When William was our King declared,
   To ease the nation's grievance,
   With this new wind about I steered
   And swore to him allegiance,
   Old principles I did revoke,
   Set conscience at a distance,
   And passive obedience was a joke,
   A jest was non-resistance
       And this is law, &c.

5. When George in pudding-time came o'er,
   And moderate men, looked big, Sir,
   I turned a cat-in-pan once more,
   And so became a Whig, Sir,
   And this preferment I procured,
   From our new Faith's defender,
   And almost ev'ry day abjured
   The Pope and the Pretender.
       And this is law, &c.

4. When gracious Anne became our Queen
   The Church of England's glory,
   Another face of things was seen,
   And I became a Tory;
   Occasional Conformists base,
   I blamed their moderation,
   And thought the Church in danger was
   By such prevarication.
       And this is law, &c.

6. The illustrious house of Hanover,
   And Protestant succession,
   To these I do allegiance swear,
   While they can keep possession,
   For in my faith and loyalty
   I never more will falter,
   And George my lawful King shall be.
   Until the times do alter.
       And this is law, &c.

Religion continued to be a point of controversy throughout the seventeenth century. Religious convictions brought out both the best and the worst in your ancestors. The first settlers in North America came for religious freedom. But they soon began to persecute those of other religious beliefs. William Brend, a Quaker, was turned away from the New World but came again in the *Woodhouse* in 1657. At Boston they laid him neck and heels in irons for sixteen hours. The next day they gave him 117 lashes. He later spent time in Newgate Prison, London, and died in that city in 1676. Other Quakers arriving in the New World were variously punished, often by the cutting off of an ear. Other religious groups were similarly persecuted.

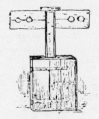

A whipping post from old Newgate prison.

Newgate Prison, 1782-1904.

Until more recent times, the local parish ministers did not care to have your Nonconformist ancestors buried in their churchyards. Very often Nonconformists were buried in fields or just over the churchyard wall or in some remote corner, as in this example from the burial registers of Christchurch, Hampshire, quoted in W.E. Tate's *The Parish Chest:*

14 April 1604 Christian Steevens, the wife of Thomas Steevens, died in childbirth and was buried by women, for she was a papishe [Roman Catholic]

In the burial of Andreas Symock in the parish of High and Low Ham in Somerset, the situation was slightly different, as this burial entry, also cited in *The Parish Chest,* explains:

This excommunicate was buried in the northern corner of the churchyard but by whom I know not

The parish registers of East Peckham, Kent, read:

1630 The papist Thomas Whettenhall buried. Entered [interred] *privately without ye minister.*

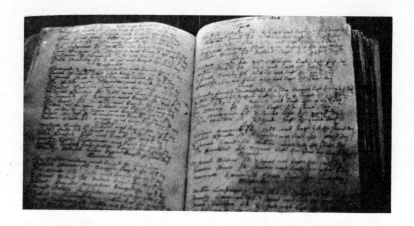

In the same parish, in 1699, John Day, an Anabaptist, was buried with a note in the register:

Excommunicated and buried under the wall without the churchyard between the gate and the walnut tree.

These are typical of many such entries in the century of much religious turmoil.

The parish church, however, witnessed more than just scenes of strife. Among the more joyous events that transpired there were our ancestors' marriages.

Some things have changed but little over the centuries, and the relationship betweeen men and women is one of them. In the 1970s its sometimes difficult to tell a boy from a girl by the way they dress. Believe it or not, Samuel Pepys had the same trouble back in 1666. He writes in his diary:

> *Walking in the galleries at Whitehall I find the Ladies of Honour dressed in their riding garbs, with coats and doublets with deep skirts, just for all the world like mine; and buttoned in their doublets up to the breast, with perriwigs and with hats; so that, only for a long petticoat dragging under their men's coats, nobody could take them for women in any point whatever; which was an odd sight.*

Just like some of us today, some of our ancestors followed their hearts more than their heads.

In Middlewich, Cheshire, in 1677, Marable Harding had an illegitimate child to John Doe. The will of James Harding in 1682 states, among other things, *"Kinswoman Marable Harding on condition she marry Thomas Whittingham or any honest man excepting John Doe."*

Evidently she decided not to benefit from her kinsman's will: On 23 October 1684 Marable Harding married John Doe at Middlewich.

How did these seventeenth-century romances begin? Many of our ancestors met at the market town as their parents brought their farm produce to market. Thus the children from one family living, say, east of the market town would meet children living to the west of the market town. From these meetings stronger associations often ensued. Were it not for the weekly or semiweekly trip to market, these ancestors may never have met each other.

Village Lock-ups at (above) Wheatley, Oxfordshire, and Panqbourne, Berkshire.

When two of your ancestors fell in love and desired to marry, how did they decide in which church to marry? Before 1837 the law said that they had to marry in the Church of England even if they were of another religion, such as Roman Catholic or Baptist. Only the Quakers were given a special privilege. Their marriages usually took place in the house of a Quaker. For the majority, however, it was the Church of England.

Which parish church would they choose? This varied widely according to the locality and the time. For example, during the time of Cromwell, when he installed many registrars in parishes instead of trained clergy, the intentions to marry were proclaimed in the market place. Many at this time would find another parish where a "genuine" minister operated, someone who, somehow, had been able to avoid eviction.

Before 1754 a couple could be married in any of the parish churches or chapels that were licensed to marry. Thus a popular minister could supplement his fees by performing extra marriages. Perhaps the countryside setting of a particular church was more romantic than others. The architecture and fabric of another church might be more appealing. After 1754, couples were supposed to marry in the parish of the bride or groom unless they obtained a special license to marry elsewhere. (See David E. Gardner and Frank Smith, *Genealogical Research in England and Wales,* 3 vols. [Salt Lake City: Bookcraft, 1956-64]: 146-49.)

Often parish registers reveal traits of our ancestors--not only of those whose lives were recorded, but also of those who kept the records. The parish minister or the parish clerk of Skipton, Yorkshire, must have been feeling poetical the day he recorded this marriage:

> *2 Dec 1629*
>
> *Francis Falis married Alis Walis*
> *without any malis*
> *and both of this parish*

Parish clerk at St. Peter, Bolton, Lancashire, makes his own introductions:

The following effusion appears on a leaf preceding the marriage for 1632 in the second Register Book:-

This part conteynes the married state
Wth most, there followes quick debate
If fortune smile then are the gladd
If not, they greeve they weare so madd
p. me Ro: Welsh

On the fly leaf preceding the Burial entries for 1632, in the second Register Book are written the following lines

This part of Booke it doth conteyne
Those dead, yett sure, must ryse againe
There names thow sees, & soe haue I.
Then Letts prepare vs both to dye.
p. me: Ro: Welsh.

Had your ancestors shared Robert Welsh's pessimistic view of life, they may have turned to drink. As it was, they probably did consume considerable quantities of alcohol. But it is not surprising that they drank large amounts of ale and other homemade brews when one considers how foul much of the water tasted.

Millions of gallons of ale were drunk every year, but one could overdo it, just as some do today. This is evidenced by an entry in Spondon, Derbyshire, parish register: *"William Hatton, a stranger, died by drinking 20 pints of ale."*

All over England, for several centuries, justices of the peace, with the aid of others, kept law and order and made judgments. It seems to have been a successful method.

If there had been newspaper reporters available in these centuries they would have spent much of their time at the quarter sessions courts, held every three months in all the large towns and boroughs, where justices of the peace heard a wide variety of complaints and problems. Many of the situations described in this book went through the quarter sessions courts. Had there been newspapers reporters, they could have obtained all they needed for their daily issues from these courts.

Here is an example of some of the things handled at the quarter session court in Surrey in 1689/90, as recorded in the Surrey Estreat Books, printed in *Surrey Records,* vol. 5:

We present Mary Bayley liueing att the Lodge in Winchester Yard in St. Saviours parish for keeping a disorderly house.

We present his Grace the Lord Arch Bishop of Canterbury for not repaireing his part at the Wharfe att Stone Gate for the space of three Rods.

That William Burditt liueing at the Cock and Crown in the Close in the parishe of St. Saviours, Southwarke, did say: 'God Damn all English men' with severall other Oaths.

Wee Present the Queen Dowager for not repaireing her part of a Bridge called Crockford Bridge being in the parish of Chersey being soe much out of repaire that their Majesties subjects are in great danger rideing that way.

William Johnson of Reigate for setting his Wagon and Carts in the street in the night the 11th December.

Wee present James Zouch Esqre for not repaireing the Stocks and Whipping Post in the Mannor of Wokeing, he being Lord of the said Manor.

Thomas Johnson of the parish of St. Olives for keeping of Lodgers which are reputed Papists haueing been warned to the Contrary.

Here are some examples taken from the Surrey sessions minute books for the year 1694, printed in the same volume:

The matter concerning Richard Coles being Reputed father of a Bastard Child begotton on ye body of Elizabeth Layton borne in ye parish of Walton-on-Thames referred to Sir James Clarke, Francis Brend Esqr and John...Esqr. or any two of them to determine ye matter and all former Orders in this matter are set aside.

The order of Mr. Hare and Mr. Ebelyn for removeing Thomas Humphrey and his wife from Abbinger to Betchworth confirmed.

Ordered on the Appeale of Albury against Sheire that Richard Peacocke bee settled att Sheire and the order of the two Justices discharged.

The Appeal of Milend about settlement of Robert Hopper and Jane his wife and four children sent from St. Thomas appears that they paid to ye scavengers and watch at St. Thomas to be sent to St. Thomas.

During several centuries many thousands of females lost their lives, condemned as witches. The interesting example that follows was taken from Essex quarter sessions at the Essex Record Office and recorded in *English History from Essex Sources: 1550-1750,* pages 39 and 40.

DUCKING A WITCH

The informacion of Rewben Bowier late of Wicken Brooke in the Countie of Suffolke singleman taken uppon oath before Christopher Muschampe Esquire one of the Justices of the Peace for the Countie of Essex the 5th daye of September, 1653.

This Informant saith That on Tuesdaye last beinge the (blank) daye of August last hee was comminge from Elsenham to Teakly in the Countie of Essex, and this Informant saith that his fathers dogge was with him, and the dogge did runne after a hogge which was John Dishes hogge of Teakly aforesaid, and that Hellen ye wife of the said John Dish, seeinge the dogge to runne after her hogge as aforesaide, did thereuppon threaten this Informant and told this Informant hee had as good not to have suffred his dogge to have worried her hogge, for hee should have noe greate joy after it. And this Informant saith that ever since Satturday morninge last, beinge the third of September instant, hee hath had exceedinge stronge & many painfull fittes to ceize on him att severall times, and that his fittes doth hold him halfe an howre or thereaboutes. And this Informant said that yesterday morninge there came a thinge uppon his bedd, like a blacke catt, and this morninge there came another thinge like a hedgehogge & satt uppon a sticke neere this Informantes bed side (hee beinge in bedd) and imediatly after the sight of those thinges, his fittes ceized on him very stronge and painfull, and he saith hee feeleth some thinge runne upp into his body whilest it comes to his throate and then hee is almost strangled & is in great torture paine & misery.

The parish constables had to report regularly at the quarter sessions court concerning the keeping of the peace. Here is the general method in which they reported, taken from the Northamptonshire quarter sessions for the parish of Creaton:

First I know non that doe profane the Lords day by cursing or swareing
I know non that are gilty of the sin of adultry or fornycation
I present William Tary (and his wife) for not coming to church nor to noe other lawfull meeting that I know of
I know non to be requsants in our parish
I know non that are of euell fame or suspect to be theeses
I know non that refuse to persue hue and crys
Wach and ward is duly keept
I know noe butcher victuallers that sell unwholsom flesh nor maulsters that seel unwholsom mault
I know non that by or sell by weight or mesures onsealed
I know non that goe about the cuntrar with countrefeit letters of request or pass.
I know non idle person that goe about the cuntry using any subtill craft or unlawfull game.
I know non that use any one lawfull game in the houses or resort to any such place that use onlawful sport.
I know noe highwaies out of repare
I know no riots or quarillars
I know non that sell ale without lisence or that break the sise of ale or beer
                    By mee John Arnoll constable of Creaton

Taxes on fireplaces were a very unpopular idea of this century. It was the job of the parish constable to see that entrance into the house was permitted so that the fireplaces could be counted and taxed accordingly. The tax was so unpopular it lasted only a few years (1662 to 1689) and was responsible for a variety of events. The following example is from Curry Mallett, a parish in Somerset:

Rich. Collier   *£ 0 6s iijd*
Shutts his doore and refuses entrance for ye halfe yeare ending at Mich. 1665.

At least the parish constable (later replaced by tax collectors called *chimney men*) was able to find out that Richard Collier had three fireplaces: The tax on each fireplace was two shillings, so the total tax for three fireplaces for that year was six shillings and three pence.

Reading like a western novel comes this story of a holdup in 1686 from the Holcroft Archives in the Essex Record Office. It is recorded in *English History from Essex Sources: 1550-1750,* pages 38 and 39:

Thomas Hunt, now a trooper in Colonel Hugh Sunderland's troop now quartered in Romford, saith that upon Monday the 12th of this instant April, about ten o'clock in the night, being sent by one of his officers to London about the troop's concerns, he hearing there that there was a post going for London, he being desirous of company made haste after him and overtook him, about one mile and a half on this side Romford, one gentleman being in company with the post boy whose name he knoweth not but hath heard that he is a merchant of London.

When the post boy and the merchant and himself came a little on this side Ilford bridge, they overtook two men, one upon a bay horse about fourteen or fifteen hands high with one white foot behind; the man had on him a pretty light coloured cloth coat, close bodied, a short, fat man with a short, brown periwig. The other man was upon an iron-grey horse about the size of the other man's; the man had upon him a close bodied cloth coat of a pretty sad colour, with slits down before for pocket holes.

The man that rode upon the bay horse took a pistol from under his coat and put it to his breast and said "Damme me, if you will not stand I will shoot you'; with that he took the informant by the hair of the head and pulled him off from his horse. The other man upon the iron-grey horse, he cut the mails off, and cut open one portmanteau and took out of it two bundles, the one was tied up in parchment the other was in a linen bag which the man on the bay horse opened, and took out of it a lesser bag and put it into his pocket. The man that was on the bay horse, hearing a noise, left this informant and met with a man driving a waggon, and bid him stand which he accordingly did. This being done he called to the man on the grey horse and said "Damme me. Will, will you not break open the other portmanteau'. He replied, 'No, Jack, let us be gone', but notwithstanding he did cut open the other portmanteau and took out of it one bundle and gave it to Jack, as he called him, but what was in it, this informant knoweth not. The informant farther saith that to his knowledge he never saw any of the two parties but believeth that if he should see one of the, that is, he that rode upon the bay horse, he should know him.

We know little about the weather in bygone centuries other than what we can glean from an occasional diary, a parish register, or estate accounts. For example, in the diary of John Evelyn he records that the winter of 1683/84 was very severe. The River Thames in London was frozen solid from December to February. Birds and fish died, and the poor had no fuel becuase it cost too much.

OWLPEN MANOR, GLOUCESTERSHIRE. The manor stands deep in a valley on the western edge of the Cotswolds near the old weaving village of Uley, and some six miles south-west of Stroud. One of the most picturesque of Cotswold manor-houses, it was built in Tudor times, and partly rebuilt in the seventeenth and eighteenth centuries.

HISTORICAL	RELIGIOUS	RECORD-KEEPING	SOCIAL, ECONOMICAL
1702 QUEEN ANNE (1702-14).			
1704 Battle of Blenheim.			
1707 United Kingdom of Great Britain formed by union with Scotland	1711- An Occasional 15 Conformity Law, aimed against the Nonconformists, passed.	1711 Order to keep parish registers with ruled and numbered pages given, but generally not observed.	
1713 Spain ceded Gibraltar to England			
1714 GEORGE THE FIRST (1714-27).	1714 Landholders compelled to take the Oath of Allegiance and renounce Roman Catholicism.	1714 Quarter sessions records from this date often mentioned Protestant dissenters and Roman Catholic recusants.	
1715 The Jacobite rebellion, during which the Roman Catholic pretender attempted to seize the throne.	1717 Roman Catholics forced by law to register their estates.		1720 Manufacturing towns increased in population. Rise of new wealth
1727 War with Austria and Spain. GEORGE THE SECOND (1727-60).	1730 The first Moravian (later also called the United Brethren) congregations established in England.		1727 Turnips first used for cattle.
1733 Proceedings in courts of justice required to be in English instead of Latin. War in Europe (Polish war).	1738 Howel Harris's sermons in Wales laid foundations for Welsh Calvinistic Methodism.	1733 Law forbidding the use of Latin in parish registers generally obeyed, although some continued in Latin for a few years.	1730s Townshend and Tull started the agricultural revolution; Kay's flying shuttle ushered in the industrial revolution.
1739 War with Spain and France.	1739 Wesley and Whitefield commenced great Methodist revival.	1738 Earliest date in known Calvinistic Methodist registers.	
	1740 John Wesley separates himself from the Moravians.	1741 Earliest date in known Moravian church registers.	

HISTORICAL	RELIGIOUS	RECORD-KEEPING	SOCIAL, ECONOMICAL
	1741 Benjamin Ingham founded the Moravian Methodists or Inghamites. George Whitefield, Calvinistic Methodist church, was preaching in London.	1741 Earliest date in known Scotch church registers in England.	
1743 40,000 English and Hanovarian soldiers were fighting in Europe.	1744 First Wesleyan Conference held.		
1745 Battle of Fontenoy. The Young Pretender, Bonnie Prince Charlie, and the Jacobites landed in Britain in an unsuccessful attempt to seize the throne.			
1746 Battle of Culloden.	1748- Countess of 56 Huntington's (Calvinistic) Methodist Connexion founded.		
		1752 New style calendar inaugurated. New year commenced on 1 January instead of 25 March. Earliest known Lady Huntington's New Connexion registers.	1750- Hargreaves designed 57 his spinning jenny.
1755 The Seven Years' War in Europe, India and America (known also as the French and Indian Wars).		1753 Earliest date in known Inghamite register.	
1757 Black Hole of Calcutta and the Battle of Plassey. The foundation laid for the Empire of India.		1754 Marriage Act (Lord Hardwicke's) to prevent clandestine marriages, passed. Ordered marriages to take place in parish of residence.	

HISTORICAL	RELIGIOUS	RECORD-KEEPING	SOCIAL, ECONOMICAL
1759 Fort Duquesne (Pittsburg) conquered by forces under George Washington.			1760 First English navigation canals.
1760 French surrendered Heights of Abraham in Canada. GEORGE THE THIRD (1760-1820).			
1762 French surrendered Canada and Florida.		1762 Earliest date in known Unitarian registers. Earliest date in known Swiss church registers	1763 Wedgewood started pottery.
1763 Peace with France.			1764-65 Early years of the industrial revolution. Watts improved his steam engine. Invention of the spinning jenny.
1765 Population of England and Wales reached seven million.	1765 Universalism preached in England.		1769 Arkwright's spinning jenny invented.
	1770 New Connexion of General Baptists organized in London.		1774-79 Crompton invented the mule.
	1773 First organized beginnings of Unitarianism in England.		1775 Water closet invented.
1776 American Declaration of Independence and the Revolutionary War.	1778 Penal Laws against Roman Catholics mitigated.	1779 Earliest date in known New Connexion Methodist registers.	
	1781 Sunday Schools founded by Robert Raikes.	1780 Earliest date in known Wesleyan Methodist registers.	1781 Trade very bad.
1783 Peace with America, France, and Spain.		1783 Duty of threepence imposed upon each entry made in the parish registers, causing some imperfect recordings.	

THE EIGHTEENTH CENTURY

HISTORICAL	RELIGIOUS	RECORD-KEEPING	SOCIAL, ECONOMICAL
1788 Settlement and colonization of New South Wales and Australia.	1788 First congregations of New Jerusalemites or Swedenborgians.	1787 Earliest date in known Swedenborgian (Church of the New Jerusalem or Jerusalemite) registers.	1785 Cartwright invented the power loom.
1789 The French Revolution.	1791 Penal laws abolished.		
1793 War with France-- 10,000 English soldiers in Flanders.	1793 Napoleonic War stopped reforms.	1794 The duty on parish register entries repealed.	
1798 Naval victories at Cape St. Vincent and Battle of the Nile.		1796 Tax on hair powder.	1797 Steam harnessed for the first time.

AN ENGLISH SUMMER DAY

Let us not disparage Autumn when the woods are red and gold
*   And Pomona is the Queen of Western Shires;*
Let us say a word for Winter when his frosty-fingered cold
*   Grips the roads that creak and crack beneath our tires;*
Let us cede her lure to Springtime when the nesting of the birds
*   In the hedges, blooming red and white with may.*
All the seasons yield us pleasure, but Enchantments fullest measure
*   Is the glory of an English Summer Day.*

Come then quickly, O Beloved! Let us wanter, you and I,
*   Listing not the trend and tending of our trail.*
Sith we go to Corfe or Craster, and we fare to Ross or Rye
*   We shall taste the old sweet charms that never fail.*
For the breeze is in the branches and the sun is high in Heaven,
*   And a magic dwells in every blade and spray.*
There's a lifting lilt of gladness that is nigh akin to madness
*   In the glory of an English Summer Day.*

On we go by town and hamlet, now the earth is half concealed
*   Neath a golden-tinted cloak of waving corn;*
Now 'tis pastureland, with cattle at their ease in every field;
*   Now 'tis heathland, studded o'er with gorse and thorn.*
Now we breast an open downland and across its ample girth
*   See our road reel out before us, far away;*
Or we walk by leafy bowers, girt with tender fragrant flowers,
*   Thro' the glory of an English Summer Day.*

But at length the day is waning and its tide is to the West
*   Let us seek a quiet inn in yonder town*
To provide us with refreshment and a place where we may rest
*   Ere the gloaming ring her crimson curtain down.*
See, yon quaint old tavern beckons and our journey has an end--
*   It is finished. Come Beloved, let us pray*
To our Father that He spare us, oft again that we may fare us
*   Thro' the glory of an English Summer Day.*

                                                    R.S.M.

(Pomona . . . the Roman goddess of fruits)

Chapter Three

THE EIGHTEENTH CENTURY

The Curfew tolls the knell of parting day,
  The lowing herd wind slowly o'er the lea,
The plowman homeward plods his weary way,
  And leaves the world to darkness and to me.

Now fades the glimmering landscape on the sight,
  And all the air a solemn stillness holds,
Save where the beetle wheels his droning flight,
  And drowsy tinklings lull the distant folds;

Save that from yonder ivy-mantled tow'r
  The moping owl does to the moon complain
Of such as, wand'ring near her secret bow'r,
  Molest her ancient solitary reign.

Beneath those rugged elms, that yew-tree's shade,
  Where heaves the turf in many a mould'ring heap,
Each in his narrow cell for ever laid,
  The rude Forefathers of the hamlet sleep.

The breezy call of incense-breathing Morn,
  The swallow twitt'ring from the straw-built shed,
The cock's shrill clarion, or the echoing horn,
  No more shall rouse them from their lowly bed.

For them no more the blazing hearth shall burn,
  Or busy housewife ply her evening care:
No children run to lisp their sire's return,
  Or climb his knees the envied kiss to share.

Oft did the harvest to their sickle yield,
  Their furrow oft the stubborn glebe has broke:
How jocund did they drive their team afield!
  How bow'd the woods beneath their sturdy stroke!

Let not Ambition mock their useful toil,
  Their homely joys, and destiny obscure;
Nor Grandeur hear with a disdainful smile
  The short and simple annals of the poor.

In addition to reading material in this chapter, it would be well worth your while to read *Tours through the Whole Island of Great Britain* (3 vols., 1724-27), by Daniel Defoe. These volumes give tremendous insight into the conditions Defoe found as he traveled. Quotes from this book on general conditions and conditions in a specific part of the country would greatly enhance the part of your family history written for this period.

The boast of heraldry, the pomp of pow'r,
  And all that beauty, all that wealth e'er gave,
Awaits alike th' inevitable hour:
  The paths of glory lead but to the grave.

. . . .

Can storied urn or animated bust
  Back to its mansion call the fleeting breath?
Can Honour's voice provoke the silent dust,
  Or Flatt'ry soothe the dull cold ear of death?

Perhaps in this neglected spot is laid
  Some heart once pregnant with celestial fire;
Hands, that the rod of empire might have sway'd,
  Or waked to ecstasy the living lyre.

. . . .

Full many a gem of purest ray serene
  The dark unfathom'd caves of ocean bear:
Full many a flower is born to blush unseen
  and waste its sweetness on the desert air.

Some village Hampden that with dauntless breast
  The little tyrant of his fields withstood,
Some mute inglorious Milton, here my rest,
  Some Cromwell guiltless of his country's blood.

. . . .

Far from the madding crowd's ignoble strife
  Their sober wishes never learn'd to stray;
Along the cool sequester'd vale of life
  They kept the noiseless tenor of their way.

Yet ev'n these bones from insult to protect
  Some frail memorial still erected nigh,
With uncouth rhymes and shapeless sculpture deck'd,
  Implores the passing tribute of a sigh.

Their name, their years, spelt by th' unletter'd muse,
  The place of fame and elegy supply:
And many a holy text around she strews,
  That teach the rustic moralist to die.

For who, to dumb Forgetfulness a prey,
  This pleasing anxious being e'er resign'd,
Left the warm precincts of the cheerful day,
  Nor cast one longing ling'ring look behind?

. . . .

For thee, who, mindful of th' unhonour'd dead,
  Dost in these lines their artless tale relate;
If chance, by lonely contemplation led,
  Some kindred spirit shall inquire thy fate,

. . . .

'One morn I miss'd him on the custom'd hill,
Along the heath and near his fav'rite tree;
Another came, nor yet beside the rill,
Nor up the lawn, nor at the wood was he;

The next with dirges due in sad array
Slow through the church-way path we saw him borne.
Approach and read (for thou canst read) the lay
Graved on the stone beneath yon aged thorn.'

THE EPITAPH

Here rests his head upon the lap of Earth
  A Youth to Fortune and To Fame unknown.
Fair Science frown'd not on his humble birth,
  And Melancholy mark'd him for her own.

Large was his bounty, and his soul sincere,
  Heav'n did a recompense as largely send:
He gave to Misry all he had, a tear,
  He gain'd from Heav'n ('twas all he wish'd) a friend.

No farther seek his merits to disclose,
  Or draw his frailties from their dread abode,
(There they alike in trembling hope repose,)
  The bosom of his Father and his God.

Thomas Gray, *Elegy in a Country Churchyard* (1750)

i. THOMAS GRAY'S TOMB, STOKE
POGIS.   (Died, 1771.)

As Gray's poem shows, the parish church preserves, for the eighteenth century as for previous centuries, not only the physical remains of "the unhonour'd dead"--our forefathers--but much of their spirit and history as well. These are often recorded in the parish registers. For example, consider the following entry from the christening register at Bishop Wearmouth, Durham:

Robert, daughter of William Thompson, bap. 15 Feb. 1730,
the midwife mistaking the sex,-she was crazed with liquor.
[Cited in Tate, *The Parish Chest,* p. 59]

Although the above is an eighteenth-century example, such a mistake in recording sex could happen in any century. On my own Smith pedigree in Suffolk I have sufficient evidence to prove that "Frances daughter of" is "Francis son of." But in that case there was no mention of a drunken midwife!

Tombstones beneath the yew trees in Stoke Rogers' churchyard as Thomas Gray saw them.

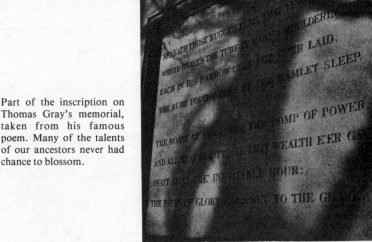

Part of the inscription on Thomas Gray's memorial, taken from his famous poem. Many of the talents of our ancestors never had chance to blossom.

Parish marriage registers are equally revealing. Here's an example of a man who had to be forced into marriage. Note that it took more than six months. This is taken from the parish registers of Isleham, Cambridgeshire.

1775 July 17 John Chapman bach. [bachelor] *of St. Trinity in the city of Ely, Cambridge, & Ursula Clarke otp* [of this parish] *by banns. Banns read 11, 18 & 25 Dec. 1774. The following note appears in the register: The said Jno. Chapman refused to set his hand or mark, alleging that he was not married: the mob threatening to duck him on his refusal that he came Shonte Sua, he alleges, likewise, that he was obliged to marry or have his brains beat out.*

As an example, the parish church of St. John in the town of Bedford recorded marriages of couples coming from almost every parish in the county. Such examples were not confined to town parishes. Tiny churches in the countryside were often just as popular. This means that when searching for the marriage of your ancestors you will have to be prepared to search in a very wide area.

Not all parish churches were the big, beautiful structures one normally sees in travel guides and calendars. Some were very quaint; some even had thatched roofs. An interesting story is told about the parish church at Flaunden in Hertfordshire. It had no regular minister, the parson or the curate walking up from Hemel Hempstead on the fourth Sunday of the month to conduct the service. If it rained or snowed, there would be no service. John Edwin Cussans, in his *History of Hertfordshire,* writes:

A party of ladies and gentlemen [who were visiting in the

neighbourhood] *walked down to old Flaunden Church . . "How very interesting," remarked one of the party, "I should so like to attend service here." "Well, to-morrow is the regular day," replied the woman who was showing them over the church, "but I do hope and trust that it will rain, and then the parson won't come, for I've got one of my best hens asitting on thirteen eggs in the pulpit, and she won't come off till Tuesday."* [3 vols. (London: *Chatto and Windus, 1879-81),* 3:179]

A Country Parson Setting Out to Visit his Parish.

The burial books in a parish often tell tragic stories. Sometimes all of a couple's children died in infancy, or perhaps one or two survived to carry on the blood line. In this and previous centuries, 60 percent of the children did not survive childhood.

In the burial entries that follow, it would appear that the family was not attending church. The minister seems to have looked upon the events as divine retribution. The parish is East Barming, Kent, in 1797:

Crouch, John, son of Thomas and Jane August 19th of a putrid fever.

Crouch, Elizabeth, daughter of Thomas and Jane, sister of the above, both of whom died of a putrid fever August 23.

Crouch, May, daughter of Thomas and Jane August 28th of a putrid fever and sister of the two preceding children.

Crouch, Thomas, son of Thomas and Jane, September 4 of a putrid fever, brother of three preceding children and by their deaths the only child of his very sorrowing parents, who by this dreadful disorder have lost all their family. Their mother was also seized with the complaint and with difficulty was saved from its malignant violence. Such a visitation seldom has happened in any family. The catastrophe has been greatly deplored. May it be influential in its effects, by awakening the dreadfully abandoned that too much abound, and who literally live without God in the world, never mentioning his sacred name but to call in question his veracity, deride his power, or to insult his Majesty by profanements, oaths, and blasphemy.

The same minister recorded another tragic death in the same year. He would have made a good modern news reporter!

Clements, Thomas, son of Richard and Isabella, January 12th. This Boy was taken ill whilst keeping in West Farleigh Parish, and was inhumanly denied a draught of cold water by the wife of one Pearson. The Bailiff finding him ill sent him home, the poor innocent fell at the commencement of his own Parish where several persons stood but had the barbarity neither to assist him nor even to inform his mother of his situation. Miss Eliz. Amhurst with that goodness that ever distinguishes her, attended to him and finding his condition went and told his case to the mother, who took him home about 5 o'clock in the evening, and he died in the night. It is melancholy to record so much hardness of heart amongst persons who would think themselves disgraced if not called Christians. Though this child was born in wedlock, he was known to have been incestuous; his uncle was his father. Shocking circumstances! (1797)

The same minister recorded other descriptions of persons who died near the parish. They give an idea how much like your ancestors you are yourself. Your ancestors wore different clothes and ate slightly different food, but their characteristics and habits are very much like those of their descendants today.

Sampson William aged 17 years and 9 months, from Leeds (Kent), son of John and Ann, March 12. by permission from the coroner. This youth caught his death in a singular manner. He was apprentice to a shoemaker. Living about half a mile from his father's house, he went with an intention of calling upon his parents but stopped at a small distance to cut two walking sticks in a small wood: having cut the sticks he was proceeding to his father's but by some means not exactly known he cut himself in a dreadful manner in his left thigh, unable to proceed leaning against a gate he had just got over, he called for assistance, a person came out of a house which stood near, but thinking him a person intoxicated he went to a neighbour that they might go together. They found him much exhausted with bleeding, but had no idea of danger ensuing from the wound, they therefore went to call his father. All this time the unhappy youth lay weltering in his blood, for he had fallen from weakness. The father thinking it right to see his son before he went for a surgeon going to him, said "William have you been drinking" to which he replied "No, father, I have not been drinking any where to day" and then instantly expired. It appears that he had put the knife with which he worked at his trade without any sheath in his pocket, which by falling, or getting over the gate struck into his thigh close to the bone and cut through arteries, sinues, and the whole of the flesh. None had supposed him in any danger until he had ceased to breath. The thigh where the wound was had been broken, but the bone was so well set that he had no lameness. The deceased bore a very good character for sobriety and propriety of conduct in other respects. The catastrophe was the most sensibly felt by his parents because they had lost a son at the same age by an injury he had received in cricketing. I feel greatly hurt to add that this youth was wicked, that he had been committing a trespass, if not a theft, nor was it the first offence. (1800)

Marshal, John aged 88 buried February 10th. This was the oldest person in the Parish: He was born in the reign of Q. Ann and lived also in those of K. Geo. i, Geo. ii and Geo. iii. He was a native of Scotland and on that account the people called him the name of Scotch, and he was better known by that than his real surname. He was bred a shoemaker, but latterly from his eyes being bad worked as a labourer. As an honest, religious, quiet man he was universally respected. He was one of the very few of the poor who not only came regularly to church on Sundays but stayed to receive the Holy Sacrament of the Lord's Supper. Latterly he was quite deaf, and so weak as to be scarce able to walk about. He had much indulged himself in his younger days in immoderate drinking, or probably he had lived longer, and in the evening of his days been stronger, for he was naturally athletic and robustly designed for longevity. He had no fault but his of drinking, and at no time did he lose his quiet, peaceable temper. (1795)

Bridgeland, William, aged 80 years. Yeoman, October 10. He was originally a servant to the Rev. James Mashborne, Rector of this Parish: He kept a Public House in Barming, East Farleigh, but latterly he resided upon a small freehold estate which he had purchased in this Parish: as he had been a Publican so he was also a sinner. Few have been so wicked; he was blasphemous, lewd, drunken, dishonest, a cruel husband, and a severe parent. I never saw him in church more than once or twice; to his other bad qualities he was one of the rudest and most incivil of men; thus abusing a good understanding -- but it pleased God in his mercy to give him a long and most severe visitation, the Bible then was his only solace and he seemed sincerely penitent for his abondoned life. May it have sealed his place.

The foregoing five examples appeared in *Local Population Studies,* no. 6.

Consumption was a common cause of death and still is in some countries. It struck one family to the ground, as recorded in the parish registers of Middleton Cheney:

> *buried 18 May 1799 Elizabeth the wife of James Smith age 29 of consumption.*
> *Mem: her maiden name was Barrett the fifth and only remaining child of her surviving father who have all died of consumption.*

Besides the usual christening, marriage, and burial entries, parish registers contain many interesting items about such things as the weather, *the price* of crops and even suggested cures for various ailments. Here is one from Sherfield on Loddon, Hampshire:

TO CURE THE RHUMATISM

Take ye inside Bark of Maiden Ash, ye inside Bark of Oak, ye inside bark of dwarf Elder. Scurvy-grass, of Wild Thyme, of Brook-lime, of each 3 handfuls a Pint of Mustard Seed, 12 Ounces of Horse-Radish, 12 Ounces of Fennel Seeds, One Ounce of Culchanell, boil all these in 4 gallons of Spring Water to three Gallons, then - Strain it off and put it to some Yeast, and let it work 48 hours then Scum ye Yeast clean off and put it into a Cask and when it hath stood 3 days, take a Small Coffee Cup first in ye Morning and one at Night & must keep from Strong Liquor and Salt Meats during the time of drinking it. A Woman with Child must not take it.

The parish clerk of Oundle, Northamptonshire, recorded events faithfully in the parish registers but in his own diary was a little more frank. The following four entries are taken from *Northamptonshire Past and Present,* vol. 5 (1976).

> *9 Apr. 1770. Today Old Ireland age 70 was married to Miss Dillingham of 25, an agreeable young lady with a Cambridge fortune.*

When it came to the administration of the Poor Law, he was equally frank:

> *Monday Dec. 16th 1776. Rogue Wheatly came into the Workhouse to-day with his wife and 4 children. He is 28 years of age and has been a lazy rogue all his life. So that he will live 50 years and Humbug the Town all the while.*
> *Friday 20th Dec. 1776. At the Town Meeting to-night at the*

Workhouse Rogue Wheatly Jawd everybody quite down and remains in the Workhouse in spite of everybody and there he will be as long as he pleases.

Very little information exists about the weather in those days outside of parish records. For 18 November 1770, the Day Book for Oundle states:

The river was in its greatest height and the land springs were so full that they burst up all the pavement opposite to my house and several people slipped in over their shoes and a woman's patten was dug out of the causeway to Edward Webster's house and great quantities of lamb earth were washed up above ground, it having been more continual heavy rain for some time past than ever was remembered by the oldest person living in England. It was almost most severly cold all the time.

Parish registers, however, are not the only source of information for family histories. These other sources--letters, tombstones, and wills--show that your ancestors, as partners and family members, loved each other just as much and possibly more so than you love each other today.

One such letter was written by Valentine Fitzhugh in 1792 to be read by his wife after his death. He died in 1800, aged 78, while serving as sheriff of Southampton. The letter begins without any formal greeting:

When you receive this, I shall be no more. However, if after this life we have any knowledge of what passes here below or have any power of aiding or assisting those of this World, my whole happiness will consist in conducting my dearest Angel to the Mansions of Eternal Bliss.

In regard to my fortune I have left you sole Mistress, because I have long since experienced your prudence, and know you will employ it to the best advantage; and likewise, as our Children are independent, it is but reasonable you should be in the same situation, for Parents can never act a more imprudent part than to make themselves dependent on them. However, as many things may not occur to you, I take the liberty to mention in what manner you may make your dispositions, agreeable to my present way of thinking; but, as circumstances may change, I do not mean to prescribe absolutely, but leave it entirely to you to act as you may think best.

As Mary is now married, and of course has a right to £ 4000 left her by her Aunt Rogers at my death and the same sum I have promised her after both our Deaths, I can only say that you will do well to leave to William and Valentine £ 4000 each, and the remainder (which will depend upon the price of

Stocks) to be equally divided between William, Valentine and Mary: but as William was so good to give us the House Furniture, I think it would be but just to leave it to him.

It is my particular desire to be buried wherever I may dye, in the plainest and least expensive manner possible, for I know nothing more absurd than to throw away money idly in transporting the dead to distant places; that (sic) twenty four hours after my Death I may be opened, my heart taken out and divided into two equal parts, each put into a silver box, one of which to be laid on my most honour'd and most dearly beloved Mother's Coffin; the other whenever my dearest Babet may dye, to be placed near her heart and buried with her; and this I intend as the last and dearest mark I can leave them of the most sincere and affectionate love I bear them.

Thus, my dearest and best beloved, I have given you my sentiments on this subject; and my last Prayer will be to Bless and preserve you happy while you remain in this World and that we may meet hereafter, to be Eternally happy and part no more. I remain with the most tenderest love, my ever dearest Angel's most affectionate Husband,

   Val. Fitzhugh

Southampton the 30 July 1792

As our son William has been so good to allow his Brother Valentine (he was stone deaf) a certain allowance yearly, and this with an intention to avoid our doing it, I thing it but right that William or his Heirs should not be prejudiced by it, wherefore, in what you may leave to Valentine, that a part may be secured, that after Valentine's Death, whatever advance William may have made Valentine may be made good to William or his Heirs.

Southampton the 1st July 1793 [Cited by Terrick Fitzhugh in ***West Surrey Borders Family History Society Magazine,*** Spring 1977]

Note the unusual request about his heart being cut into two pieces. In other cases an ancestor has requested the heart to be taken out and buried in another place.

While very few tombstones for the seventeenth century still exist in churchyards, for the eighteenth century and onwards they do. The inscriptions have always been a source of interest--some with their wry humor, and some with their very serious moods. On seeing your ancestor's inscription, you may wonder if he was really as he is described or if the stonemason or someone else devised the inscription after the ancestor died.

It is true that throughout England certain stock verses can be found, sometimes with slight variations. But there are others that have to be original. For example, at Garstang in Lancashire it cost more to be buried inside the church than it did outside. This was true everywhere, of course, but there one individual made a play on this. His tombstone is just outside the door to the parish church. The inscription reads in part:

> *Here I lie outside the church door*
> * Here I lie because I'm poor*
> *The further in the more they pay*
> * But here I lie as snug as they*

Many of your ancestors' tombstones look towards eternity in a more serious mood. Such is the one following, which expresses a genuine feeling of the minister for his wife, who is remembered in the inscription:

> *There is another and a better world*
> *A lonely prilgrim I am left in this*
> *Gods will be done, but if my prayers be heard we*
> *soon shall meet again. Till then sleep on sweet*
> *innocent! Thou stranger to offence. Thy God hath*
> *called thee and that very voice which thunders*
> *Terror through the guilty soul, With tongues of*
> *seraphs whispers peace to thine.*

There may be many reasons why one cannot find an ancestral connection, but the following story, substantiated by the tombstone inscription, is one of the more unusual:

Copy of Singular Inscription
UPON TOMBSTONE IN
MARTHAM CHURCH, NORFOLK

In the latter end of the seventeenth century there resided at the Hall, Martham, in the County of Norfolk, a Farmer, who was Lord of the Manor, and a person of position in the district.

He had a daughter named Alice, aged seventeen years, who through an incestuous intercourse with him gave birth to a son. To hide the disgrace and prevent its becoming generally known, the child was taken away and placed in the Foundling Hospital. Attaining the allotted age for leaving that institution, he was put out and employed in agriculture when, after a series of years, and in the course of his wanderings for employment, he came to the village of Martham. The lady, who by death of father and mother, had become possessed of the farm, required a labourer, and upon his applying to her was engaged in that capacity. By perserverance, steady habits, and industry, he rose from the position of labourer to Steward or Farm Bailiff, and by his successful management of the property, his Mistress was induced to become his Wife. His position as master of the Hall raised him to the office of Churchwarden (see bell in steeple, Christopher Bunaway). One Sabbath morning he was changing his linen, when Alice, his wife, inadvertently entered his bedroom, observed a peculiar mark on his shoulder, and she immediately recognised him as her offspring. She was so struck with horror that she fainted. Upon recovering consciousness she was just able to explain to her husband the fact, but the shock was too much for her, and she never left the chamber alive. The effect upon him was so great that he gradually sank and expired a few months afterwards, requesting that the following inscription should mark their resting place, and the incident which so unexpectedly terminated their lives.

Here Lyeth the Body of

Christopher Bunaway,

Who departed this life
ye 18th day of October, anno domini,
1730

Aged 59 Years.

And there Lyeth

Alice,

Who in her life was my Sister,
my Mistress, my Mother,
and my Wife.

Died February 12th, 1729.

Aged 76 Years.

In 1856, in consequence of the Restoration of the Church, the slabs were removed to the Church tower, and are partially obscured by the Organ being placed over them, but sufficient remains to the public view to shew a portion of the inscription.

The Stage Coach, the principal vehicle of travel before the advent of the railway.

Hackney Coach. 1720.

Shop Front, Haymarket, London, 1720.

Wills are another excellent source of information about your ancestors. While it is true that only a small percentage of adults left wills, one should not give up too easily. Wills have been found for so-called paupers, for weavers, and even for miners; so one cannot say without searching that an ancestor did not leave a will.

Here is an eighteenth-century will which would be very valuable in compiling a family history of the Parrott family:

Will of Robert Parrot in the Peculiar Court of Snaith, Yorkshire

Dated the 4th of January 1781

IN THE NAME OF GOD AMEN, I ROBERT PARROT of Reedness in the Parish of Whitgift in the County of York, Mariner, being in good health and of sound mind and memory, praised be to God for the same, I make, publish and declare this my last Will and Testament in manner and form following, that is to say, FIRST, I do hereby Give and Devise unto my son Joseph Parrot at my decease all that my house fronting the street and kitchen adjoining wherein he now dwells to him his heirs and assigns forever. And I do hereby give and bequeath unto my son Joseph Parrot aforesaid all that my sloop whereon he now sails as Master called the Robert and Rebecca he paying all her debts. I also charge my son Joseph Parrot aforesaid with the payment of three pounds a year out of the house and sloop aforesaid unto my wife Rebecca Parrot his mother during the term of her natural life the first payment to be made twelve months after my decease and so on yearly and every year during the term of her natural life.

SECONDLY, I do hereby give and devise unto my son THOMAS PARROT at my decease all that my house wherein I now dwell adjoining to and being south of the above named house to him his heirs and assigns forever. And I do hereby give and bequeath unto my son Thomas Parrot aforesaid all that my sloop whereon he now sails as Master called the Good Intent he paying all her debts. I also charge my son Thomas Parrot aforesaid with the payment of three pounds a year out of the house and sloop last above named unto my wife Rebecca Parrot his mother during the term of ther natural life the first payment to be made twelve months after my decease and so on yearly and every year during the term of her natural life.

THIRDLY, I do hereby give and devise unto my daughter ELIZABETH COOPER the wife of Joseph Cooper at my decease all that my house wherein she now dwells adjoining to and being south of the last above named house during the term of her natural life and at her decease to my son Benjamin Parrot his heirs and assigns forever.

FOURTHLY, I do hereby give and devise unto my son Benjamin Parrot at my decease all that my other out houses adjoining to and being south of the last above named house to him and his heirs and assigns forever and I do hereby give and bequeath unto my son Benjamin aforesaid all that my sloop wherein he now sails as Master called the Peacock he paying all her debts. I also charge my son Benjamin Parrot aforesaid with the payment of two pounds a year out of the out houses and sloop last above named unto my wife Rebecca Parrot his mother during the term of her natural life the first payment to be made twelve months after my decease and so on yearly and every year during the term of her natural life.

FIFTHLY, I do hereby give and devise unto my three sons aforesaid at my decease, that is to say, Joseph Parrot, Thomas Parrot and Benjamin Parrot all that my earth or yard adjoining all the above named houses to be equally divided among them each to have share and share alike for the use and convenience of each others buildings above named to them their heirs and assigns forever.

SIXTHLY and lastly, I DO HEREBY GIVE AND BEQUEATH at my decease all the rest residue and remainder of my personal estate goods and chattles of what nature or kind soever after payment of my debts and funeral expenses unto my dearly beloved wife Rebecca Parrot and my son Benjamin Parrot aforesaid whom I do hereby make nominate constitute and appoint sole and joint Executrix and Executor of this my last Will and Testament hereby revoking all and every other will and wills by me at any time heretofore made.

IN WITNESS WHEREOF I have hereunto set my hand and seal this Fourth day of January in the year of our Lord

ONE THOUSAND SEVEN HUNDRED AND EIGHTY ONE.

(signed) ROBERT PARROT

signed, sealed, published and declared by the above named Robert Parrot the testator as and for his last Will and Testament in the presence of us who in his presence and at his request and in the presence of each other have subscribed our names as witnesses hereto.

ANN SHEPPERD
JOHN SHEPPERD
THOMAS ELLAS

The within named Executrix, Rebecca Parrot, was duly sworn before me.

March 13th 1783   *Edw. Bracken, Surr:*
_____ *24th March 1783*

As you analyze this will you will note that there are a number of interesting items that would enhance a written family history--information probably not obtainable elsewhere. Let's look at them:

1. Robert Parrot was a mariner. He lived in that part of the parish of Whitgift, Yorkshire, called Reedness.
2. He had three sons--Joseph, Thomas, and Benjamin.
3. He had a sloop called the *Robert and Rebecca* (Rebecca is his wife's name). another one called the *Good Intent,* and another called the *Peacock.*
4. He had a daughter Elizabeth who married a Joseph Cooper.

As in previous centuries, the care of the poor was a major concern. This century saw the establishment of many workhouses to give employment to the poor.

The workhouse at Diss, Norfolk, was begun in 1728 from several almshouses then in existence. The following description of it is from *Waveney Valley Studies,* by Eric Pursehouse.

> The workhouse had 29 named rooms or compartments, including four 'out-door'. A Master administered it-not a trained social worker, but one who "contracted" to run it under an agreement with the churchwardens and overseers who formed the nucleus of the house committee.
>
> He had his "study", with its "book case and shelves" containing personal records of inmates, vagrants, casuals, and those receiving out relief. He had his "Keeping Room", or parlour equipped with a "30-hour clock, range and coal shoot", but he also enjoyed the use of the large committee room, with its "12 hollow seated elm chairs, two elbow chairs, oval table with green baize cloth, and stove".

Here the wardens, overseers, doctors and constables held their monthly deliberations and settled "Requests at the House"-the multitude of applications for out relief, which reflect the poverty of the age.

For obstreperous customers, there was a "Dark Room" for temporary confinement and cooling off (no furniture in this) and for the really tough a prison containing just a straw bed, but fitted with padlock and key.

The Master's deputy was quartered in the Page's Room-with "stump bedstead, mattress and chair".

Feeding was communal-in a large "Dining Room" sparsely furnished with "four tables, eight forms, 23 earthenpans, 22 wooden dishes, a Dutch oven, a coal range and Brass Boiler".

Workhouse fare consisted of three meals-for breakfast, bread with either gruel, meat broth or pease pottage; for dinner, meat with suet or plain puddings, or dumplings, bread and small beer; or, for variation, milk broth and bread, or pease pottage and small beer; and for supper just bread, cheese, and small beer, every night.

This delightful and varied food was prepared in the "kitchen" (with broth ladle, dumpling stirer, three coppers, lids and furnaces)-the "Baking Office" (with kneading trough, meal hutch, bushel and strike, and scales)-the "Soup House" (with soup copper, lid and furnace, and even a swill-tub).

For idling away their time the inmates had three day rooms- "The Middle Room", for general use, with "benches, chairs and stools"; the men's "Low Room", with "old men's settle"; and the "Widow's Room", with seven chairs, candlesticks and a tinder-box.

Sleeping accommodation was provided for 29 in five "wards" and sick-ward-the women's ward with its seven bedsteads, one chair, five coverlets, ten blankets and ten sheets, being the largest.

Under his contract the Master could use his inmates profitably-hence the "Taylor's shop" with "Taylor's Board, Goose, and sundry old pieces of clothes" for repairs-and the "Laundry" with mangle, ironing boards, box and flat irons-and the "Weaving shop" with two looms, winding wheel and warping bar-where hemp was spun and hempen cloth woven. (26 bundles of hemp were in store).

Thirty spinning wheels were stored in the "attics"-for loan to outpatients on request. "Slops" and boys' jackets were also stored there in profusion.

The contents of the store room reflected both the contemporary clothing materials of the poor, and the products of local industry-40 yards of shirt and shift cloth, 37 yards of sheeting, 70 sheets and shifts, five yards of stay-stuff (all of course hempen cloth)-with 22 yards of Duffield, 80 yards Wolsey, 43 old Wolsey dresses, 12 pairs women's and 12 of men's stockings, 26 flannel petty-coats and 18 yards flannel. (All coarse woolen materials).

Wool spinning, weaving, and the making of hosiery still lingered in Diss-and many "wool wheels" were out on loan from the Workhouse.

No reference is made in the inventory to washing or bathing facilities-apart from coppers. Life was hard and certainly unhygienic.

However, at the time of the inventory (1834), the erection of the Union Workhouse at Pulham was about to begin. It was completed 1836-7, to accommodate 500 inmates, with provision for employment of the able-bodied. It was then that Diss Workhouse was reconverted to the Almshouses.

There was a workhouse at Alfreton as early as 1747. John Newbold, mentioned in the following bill, must have been a supplier of tailoring materials such as pins, needles, thread, flannel, laces, holland, tape, dimity, etc.

Alfreton 9ber 23 1746[/7]

Bo[ugh]t of John Newball for the poor
of the worke house of Alfreton

		£ s d
	Scotch Th[read]	0 . 0 . 0½
9ber 28 :	pins	0 : 8 . 0½
9ber 30 :	½ z of Cotton Th[read]	0 : 0 : 1
apy	½ the Laces 23 blew Inkle 1 Needels	0 : 0 : 3½
ap 2 :	1 y[ar]d of flannil	0 : 1 : 0
	¾ of Ditto 10 : 1 y[ar]d of Holland 11	0 : 1 : 9
	2½ y[ar]ds ½ y[ar]d of Dimmothea at 12	0 : 0 : 7½
	Tapes . Th[read] 1	0 : 0 : 2
9ber 3 :	thrid	0 : 0 : 1
5	Stocken Needels	0 : 0 : 0½
9ber 18	pins	0 : 0 : 1
		£0 : 4 : 2½

Rec[eive]d the 21 Ap 1747 the above Contents
£0 : 4 : 2½

In full J John Newball

A Farmer, 1780-1815
the most properous
years for agriculture.

A Georgian Squire. Typical
country landowner and
magistrate.

Concerning the operation of the Poor Laws and the relief of the poor, there were several attempts during the 18th century to tighten things up still further. In 1753, for example, there was an attempt to deny relief to anybody who declined to enter a workhouse. The same Act, incidentally, empowered parishes to unite to form Unions to build and share a workhouse. Right throughout the 18th century there was considerable litigation between parishes. It was an extremely expensive operation. Parishes would claim that someone was not entitled to relief; they would appear before a Justice to be examined; their legal place of settlement would be discovered; they would be sent there and maybe the receiving parish refused to accept them. All their efforts seemed to be concentrated on avoiding the payment of relief.

There was much concern about the prevention of vagrancy, and in 1743/44 a reward of five shillings was introduced for removing any vagrants to their legal place of settlement, after whipping. Incorrigible rogues were treated far more harshley--imprisonment, with whipping at the Justice's discretion, and they were either sent home or pressed into naval or military service. Persons found sheltering vagabonds were fined from 10/- to 40/-, a lot of money in those days. One important modification made was that the bastard child of a vagrant woman would have its mother's place of settlement. This, in fact, was a humane act, for pregnant women had been hastened on from parish to parish to make sure that the baby would be born under someone else's haystack. A high proportion of mothers and children died with this sort of treatment, and this had become something of a scandal. There was no particular reason to hurry the mother on because the baby would have her place of settlement anyway. What place that was often had to be established. Another slightly humanizing amendment in 1781/82 was that no poor were to be sent to a workhouse which was more than 10 miles from their own parish and no children less than 7 years old forcibly separated from their parents; in 1792 no female vagrant was to be whipped. [Donald J. Steel, from a lecture recorded in the *Bedfordshire Family History Society Journal,* vol. 1, no. 6 (Summer 1978)]

All expenses incurred in looking after the poor of each parish were recorded in the account book of the church warden. Entries in these strike home to the very heart of daily living.

For example, the account book for the small parish of Puxton in Somerset has this entry for 6 December 1788:

Let Grace Lovell have 13 qts of Brandy at 21p qt		*01*	*06*	*00*
do	*1 gallon of wine*	*00*	*07*	*00*
10 Dec 1788				
pd for a Coffin for Grace Lovell		*00*	*13*	*00*
do for wool		*00*	*03*	*00*
do pd towards the funeral		*00*	*04*	*00*

pd Dr Norman his bill	02	06	00
pd Phebe Ridler for attending Grace Lovell	00	17	00

Poor Grace Lovell must have been in extreme pain with whatever illness she had. It is assumed that the brandy and wine were used as drugs to help alleviate the pain.

Parish registers contain many references to the wearing of badges by the poor. For example, the vestry minute book of Burton-on-Trent, Staffordshire, 6 September 1702 reads:

Whereas several persons that receive alms out of the poore's levy of this liberty do often omitt the wearing of the public badge of this town or observe the same--

It is therefore ordered that when any such poore person or persons shall, or their children, bee seen without such badge or to observe the same that upon the view of either of the overseers or reliable information thereof to them of the neglect of wearing or observing such badge, such poore person or persons shall for a fortnight thenafter lose his and their allowance out of the poore's levy and the like penalty shall be continued so often as any such offence shall be committed, and not put in pay again till such badge be worn.

Apparently many refused to obey the order. For example, it was ordered on 6 June 1703, *that Elizabeth Salisbury, Mary Budworth, Hannah Scott, and Ann Hinckley be taken out of the constant pay on their stubborn refusal to wear the badge publicly.*

And in the same parish, dated 10 December 1749:

Whereas great numbers of vagrants and sturdy beggars have for some time past frequented this town, and for preventing the same for the future it is ordered that Robert Hinds be allowed 25s. quarterly for the care and pains in looking after and driving out of the town all vagrants and beggars both by night and day.

Many miles away is a similar example. The municipal records of Liverpool, Lancashire, dated 13 May 1685, read:

Ordered that all persons whose names are in the Poore Book, and who receave almes in this burrough shall weare a pewter badge wth ye towne's armes engraved on it, and such as refuse to weare them are hereby ordered not to have anie releife from this towne.

About 1775, the parish authorities of Birmingham, Warwickshire, decided to compel persons receiving relief to wear badges, and had a number of badges cast for this purpose. *An old woman,* says Roberts, in his *Social History,*

was the first brought before the board, who told her what the order was, and gave her the badge of disgrace. She courtesied, and expressed her readiness to do as they commanded without delay. Pulling up her gown, she pinned it on her petticoat; then letting fall her gown, the badge was invisible, and thus the plan was frustrated, to the great annoyance of the parish law makers.

As a contrast to the above, read the following notices, drawn from *Williamson's Liverpool Advertiser* for 1759:

Liverpool, May 25.--On Tuesday last was married at Hale, Dr. Zachariah Leafe, of Prescot, to Miss Martha Clough, of Halewood, an agreeable young lady of 18 years of age, with a very genteel fortune.

July 13. Married on Sunday last, Mr. Edward Bailey to Mrs. Hannah Knight, a widow, with a handsome fortune.

Sept. 21 On Thursday, 13th inst., at Kendal, in Westmoreland, Colonel George Wilson, to Miss James, of Kirkby Stephen, an agreeable young lady, with a fortune of 14,000 pounds. Last week, at the same place, John Heyes, M.D., to Miss Smyth, an accomplished lady, with a considerable fortune. Also,

On Sunday last, the 16th instant, Mr. John Cummins, an eminent hosier, to Miss Betty Newby, a genteel lady, with a fortune of £ 900.

As in every century, there were some colorful characters who found ways to enjoy some of the privileges of the wealthy while still belonging to the poorer classes. Such a character was the woman described below. She was definitely one of the more colorful characters of the eighteenth-or any other-century.

"We hear from Rye in Sussex, that a woman, about 24 years of age, of a brown complexion, having a scar at the corner of her right eye, and mole on the ball of her right thumb, who has gone by the several names of Charlotte Aislaby, alias Vernon, alias Waller, alias Millbank, alias Clarissa Montague, alias Kitty Carpenter, alias Charlotte Goare, alias Charlotte the wife of Edmund Wright, alias Kitty Charlotte St. Quintin, alias Mary Blieth, alias Charlotte, the Wife of ----- Shoveler, has travelled about the Country pretending to be related to several of the Nobility, and principal Commoners in this Kingdom, and by such pretensions, and many other artifices, has not only obtained relief from many unwary persons, but otherwise greatly imposed on them. In February last she came to Rye, where she pretended to be the youngest Daughter of a noble Earl, and that she had eloped from her Father's Seat with a Soldier: She desired the Magistrates to write to her Father to take her home, and to others of the Nobility (whom she pretended to be acquainted with) to intercede with her Father on her behalf, for which Imposition, and for several acts of Vagrancy, she was committed to the House of Correction till the Sessions, when she refusing to give an account of herself, was adjudged an incorrigible Rogue, and sentenced to be imprisoned for six Months, and during her Confinement to be publickly whipt three Times; And the first of this Month she received her last punishment and was discharged. We are told this Woman for like Offences has been imprisoned at Chelmsford, Dartford, Canterbury, and many other places, and has been married to no less than thirteen Husbands, many of whom are living." [From the *Sussex Weekly Advertiser or Lewes Journal* for 6 Oct. 1760, in the *Genealogists' Magazine* 19, no. 3 (Sept. 1977): 90]

Through the centuries, our male ancestors are found being called on to defend the realm, not necessarily as regular servicemen but as local militia. The following statements are taken from the Introduction to a book called Northamptonshire Militia Lists 1777, edited by Victor A. Hatley and printed for the Northamptonshire Record Society in 1973:

> Liability to serve in the militia rested on able-bodied men between the ages of 18 and 45 years. However, peers of the realm, clergymen (including dissenting ministers), articled clerks, apprentices, seamen and parish constables were exempt. So also were poor men who had three or more children born in wedlock, a number which was reduced to one in 1786. Service in the militia was for three years and determined by ballot, but any man whose name was drawn had the right to provide a substitute.

Then follows a list of men, by name and occupation, each within their respective parish of residence, each parish within its civil division called a hundred. Names from two parishes follow, giving an idea of the men available in each parish just prior to the declaration of war with France in March 1778:

CHAPEL BRAMPTON

A list of the mens names that are qualifi'd to serve in the militia of ye parissh of Chapple Brampton.

James King, grazier
Willm. Clever, farmer
James Cook, servant
Henry Judg's, servant
Bartlet Miller, farmer
Wilm. Spencer, laberour
John Spencer, servant
Stephen Hadden, servant
John Hammon, laberour
Henry Maine, butcher
John Wissh, blacksmith
Benjamen Knight, shoemaker
Edwd. Tarry, shoemaker
Robert Litchfeild, farmer
Richard Bray, miller
Thos. Brewer, laberour

(Willm. Hammon, laberour, not sharp)
(Nathil. Green, shoemaker, drawn)
(James Morris, ragman, lame)
(Henry Crutchly, shoemaker, seven children)
(John Litchfield, farmer, very bad health)
(William Litchfield, farmer, drawn)
(Edwd. Hogden, labourer, four children)
(Thos. Moird, butcher, drawn)
(John Bradshaw, shoemaker, not sound)

Edwd. Sherman, constable.

CHURCH BRAMPTON

Church Brampton. A list of all persons between the ages of eighteen and fourty five lieable to searve in the millita —— 1777.

Edwd. Carr, farmer
(Willm. Baringer, do.)
Edwd. Baringer, do.
Willm. Pain, do.
Willm. Clarke, servt.
Willm. Cox, do.
Thos. Winter, do.
Vinct. Shortland, do.
Thos. Cruft, do.
Henry Summerfield, do.

Henry Webb, do.
(Josh. Higason, albr., 5 childn.)
(John Bauldwin, do., 3 childn.)
(Wm. Brightman, do., 4 childn.)
(James Neeal, do., 6 childn.)
(Saml. Tarry, do., 3 child.)
(John Tarry, drawn once)
(Wm. Rigby, drawn once)
(Wm. Sharpe, drawn once)
(John Camp,, drawn once)

Willm. Ashby, do.
George Walker, do.
Josh. Fancutt, labr.
John Tarry, labr.
Benjn. Rigby, do.
Robt. Ingram, do.
Thoms. Tarry, wool comber
Josh. Sharpe
Charles Fancutt, farmer

(Wm. Roe, dischargd. soldier,
   lame, quit last time)
(John Webb, lame four finger)
(Wm. Bradshaw, taylor, hath
   fits, 5 child.)
(John Tutchinor, wool comber,
   hath the rumaties)
(Wm. Esom, weaver, one eye
   blemished, quit last time)
(Robt. Carr, constable.)

The escorting of poor persons from their parish on the way back to their parish of legal settlement was sometimes an unpleasant task. The parish constable escorted them to the constable of the next parish en route to their home parish so that several constables would be involved before the unfortunate persons arrive at their home parish. The following example is taken from volume 1 of *Genealogical Research in England and Wales,* page 136:

"The examination of **Martha Burnett** *rogue and vagabond apprehended by* **Ye Constable of Aylesbury** *in the County of BUCKS and brought before me, one of His Majesty's Justices of the Peace for the County of* **Bucks** *aforesaid, And Taken before Me this 18th day of April in the year of our Lord 1760."*

Then follow instructions to convey Martha Burnett and her three-week-old daughter to Tilehurst, Berkshire, where she had her settlement . . . In order to convey her from Aylesbury, Bucks, to Tilehurst in Berks, she was handed from parish to parish along the route, and she probably had to walk all the way. The document shows that from Aylesbury she was moved to Thame, the first large parish along the route.

"To the Constable of Thame in the Co. of Oxford. Convey the within named Vagrant to Wallingford in the County of Berks"

On the back of the document are handwritten endorsements by the officials who each in turn saw to the conveyance along the route.

"To the constables of the Borough of Wallingford. Convey the within named Vagrants to Cholsey in the Co. of Berks.

"To the constables of Cholsey in the County of Berks. Convey the within named vagrant from Cholsey aforesaid to the parish of Tilehurst."

So the poor woman and her three-week-old child arrived in Tilehurst, was delivered to the Constable, and the document shows that the child born near Aylesbury, Bucks., is connected with the parish of Tilehurst, Berks., the place of settlement of Martha Burnett.

While the poor were often forced to travel from place to place, others chose to lead a nomadic life.

From about 1700 onwards, gypsies traveled the countryside in their elaborately decorated caravans.

Gypsies are common all over Europe and are believed to have come originally from Egypt. Entries in parish registers will sometimes have the word *gypsy* or *Egyptian* added, as in this example from Weston by Welland, Northamptonshire:

born 13 Apr baptised 17 April 1791 Samuel Smith, gipsies.

Their language--Romany--is believed to be based on a northwest Indian dialect. They earned their living by fortune-telling and loved to play string instruments. Inside their caravans they had a type of Queen Anne stove, but in good weather they did all their cooking outside.

Some of the ones I knew as a boy were poachers and could not be trusted generally, but doubtless there were different classes among them. They were a colorful part of the English scene. The surname *Smith* seems to have been very common among them.

They never stayed long in one place as a general rule. If you have gypsy ancestry, it could be very hard to trace because of their love to roam.

Many of your ancestors clung to the Roman Catholic faith after the church had been suppressed by penal law. In 1745 Bonnie Prince Charlie (of the House of Stewart) attempted to seize the throne, as had his father before him in 1715. In the example that follows, there is evidence--among other events being described, such as caring for the poor--of restrictive measures being taken against papists. This example is taken from East Ham constables accounts for 1743 and reprinted in *Some Examples of English Handwriting* (Essex Record Office). (East Ham was not far from London so would be involved in the making of national history.)

y^e	To Caring thet Madman away	0	5	0
Oct^{br}. 1	To a Return of the Coppyholders & paid Gouge	0	5	0
	To takeing Nann Taylor and keeping her all Night	0	2	0
Nov^{br} 19	To A Return	0	2	0
Jan^{ry} 7	To A Return	0	2	0
	To takeing old Nann to Barking	0	1	0
y^r 11	To takeing up Nann Cox and her two Daughters	0	5	3
	Expended at M^r. Jerseys with Ditto	0	13	6
J. 14	To Caring A man to barking that stole a Wigg .	0	1	0
March 10th	To A Return of the papists	0	1	6
24	To Swareing & Sumensing one papist to Ilford . .	0	1	6
	Paid for Thos. Thomlinson Coppy	0	2	0
31	To A Return	0	2	0
Ap^{il}. 3	To Billiting out the Soldiers	0	1	0

The parish constable's accounts and the churchwarden's accounts read somewhat like our local newspapers. We can get a good idea from these sources of what was going on in a parish or county by using these sources. Here is one from Northamptonshire:

1718. Sep. I. Expenses with Henry Soam about having him   £ s. d.
before the Justices for refusing to lodge travellers

1719. June 9. Expenses having Goody Whitmill before the Justices for pulling Mrs. Woolf's hay

1720. May 21. Paid at Edgcote to Mr. Chauncey's Clerk for warrant to have Ann Whitmill before the Justices for selling of ale without a License 0 0 6

Dec. 16. A Levy made by James Blinco for raising £ 5 8 6 laid upon the parish of Farthinghoe by Mr. Frewen of Brackley's Robbery. His losses and charges £98 13 5 which was in King Sutton hundred committed

1721-2. Mar. 30. Paid to 2 Watchmen to Guard 2 Women all night that threatened to break all the windows in town because I could not get them lodging 0 2 0

May 7. Paid for warrant which the Justices sent to Mrs. Woolf to come to Thrupp to shew cause why she refused to pay the Window tax on Sir John Egerton's house

The work of the parish constable was, for the most part, unpleasant. Each adult male took a yearly turn at the assignment, although he could hire someone to take his place. The example below shows the effort made to recover a stolen horse. Theft was taken seriously because the owner could have a fine levied against the Hundred (a civil division within the county) in which the robbery took place. *Hue and cry* meant pursuit of anything, not necessarily a horse.

Essex   To the Constable of Orset
*   A brown bay Horse between 13 & 14 hands high with*
*   two white feet behing & many white sadle galls in*

*both sides of back with a wisk tayl & some white hairs
on the off side of his main & abought 12 years of age
being stole out of the grounds of William Philps of
west Tilbury in the County of Essex Clerk this last
night aprill ye 25th: 1728 these air therefore in his
Maiesteis name to requier you to make Hue & Cry
after the said horse & further to act & do as the law
directs --*

John Tomlin Constable
of West Tilbury

*this is to go to Brentwood & so to Epping & so past
Brentwood ye 26th Instant AP^r|* [from More Examples
of English Handwriting]

If your ancestor was a parish constable, he had to report
regularly to the court of quarter sessions (a tri-monthly court of the
county and of large towns) that watch and ward were being duly
kept.

Serious infractions of the law reached the county assizes. One
can well imagine the plight and desperation of those listed below

—TIMBER-STEALING RIOTS IN WHITTLEBURY AND SALCEY
FORESTS, IN 1727-28

A List of the Persons names wch. were bound over to the Assizes for
unlawfully cutting down and carrying away sev^{ll}. trees out of the Forests of
Salcey and Whittlewood belonging to his Mtie.

Neither Heyford . . . 9	persons	Grimscott 4		persons
Milton 5	"	Whittlebury 2		"
Gayton 3	"	Perry End & Heaven-		
Roade 3	"	cutt 2		"
Shitlanger 7	"	Maidford 2		"
Stoke Brewen 5	"	Alderington 2		"
Weston & Weedon. . 2	"	Abthorpe 2		"
Helmdon 3	"	Passenham cum Dun-		
Mourton Pinkany. . 1	"	shanger 3		"
Collingtree 13	"	Causegrave 3		"
Courteenhall 4	"	Wooburcutt 1		"
Ashton 3	"	Yardley Gobion . . . 2		"
Hartwell 5	"	Potterspury 3		"
Bradwin 3	"	Ensoutt & Asoutt . . 4		"
Wappenham. 3	"	Whitfield 3		"
Soulgrave 3	"	Blakesley 2		"
Falcutt 2	"	Silveston 3		"
Slapton 3	"	Syresham 5		"
Grafton Regis 3	"	Adson 2		"
Wicken 3	"	Greens Norton 3		"
Paulerspury 4	"	Farthingstone 1		"
Brackley 2	"	Towcester 5		"
Woodened 3	"	Hulcott 1		"

[*Northamptonshire Notes and Queries,* p. 197]

Smuggling continued through the centuries. Because of the lack of mass communications, the colorful news of such events was usually confined to the inhabitants of the·immediate area where the events occurred.

Many of the local people were in some way connected with smuggling since it helped them in the constant struggle to make ends meet. Here is an unfortunate example of where lives were lost:

Smugglers creeping warily inland, leading heavily-laden horses.

The most gruesome of all the outrages committed by the smugglers at this time resulted in the murders of a Customs officer and of an informer. A number of smugglers who had had tea seized from them by a revenue cutter broke open the Custom House at Poole and carried away a large quantity of tea. On the 6 February 1747 Mr. Till, the Collector of Chichester, told the Board of Customs that John Diamond (alias Dimer), one of the persons concerned in the affair had been apprehended and committed to gaol. The Commissioners instructed Mr. Till to find the informer Daniel Chater and have him sent to Chichester to Mr. Battine, Surveyor General of Sussex, who would arrange for Diamond's committal. The Collector of Southampton arranged for an officer, William Galley, to accompany Chater to Chichester. By the 20th of February the two men had still not arrived at Chichester and it was feared that some mishap had befallen them. Eventually the Commissioners instructed the Southampton Collector to offer a reward for information about Chater and Galley.

In due course informants came forward and arrests were made. It appeared that on the way to Mr. Battine's residence they had called at a public house for refreshment. The landlady was suspicious and warned some smugglers of their presence. The latter managed to get hold of the letter which the two men were carrying to Mr. Battine and realized what it would mean if Chater were allowed to give evidence against Dimer. They seized the unfortunate men and lashed them with whips. Other smugglers who had been concerned in the Poole raid arrived and, after some discussion, it was decided that the two should be done away with, whereupon they were tied to a horse and taken into the country. All the while the two men were lashed pitilessly until at length Galley died. Chater managed to survive a little longer, but eventually he was taken to a dry well and hung there and, to make sure he was really dead, the smugglers threw earth and stones on him. In due course six men were charged with these murders and were condemned to death, the bodies of all but two of them being hung in chains. [From Carson, *The Ancient and Rightful Customs*]

Many of your ancestors, however, may not have been involved in such dramatic events. Most probably belonged to the working classes. After the harvest each year, your working-class ancestor might have been found making his services available at a *hiring session.* Hiring sessions originated after the Black Death of the fourteenth century, when laborers were in short supply, but were the most popular in the eighteenth century. Most towns held sessions, as did good-sized country parishes. Smaller parishes would band together in small groups for the hirings.

Waveney Valley Studies discribes such a session held at Diss, Norfolk. A large group of men and women assembled on the third Thursday in September and haggled for wages with prospective employers. The constable handled the affairs and kept a record, and sometimes "earnest money" changed hands.

As it was necessary to make sure that each person being hired had legal settlement somewhere, examinations of settlements were recorded. Here is an example:

Henry Sillett, gardener, entered the service of Sarah Smith, a widow, of Diss, in pursuance of an hiring at Diss Petty Sessions, 1760 for one whole year, at 5 quineas yearly, and 2s6d hiring money.

A record such as this, relating to an ancestor, could be very valuable.

We do not hear too much about coal mining and coal miners in the eighteenth century, so I was grateful to read about the following incident involving coal miners from Kingswood, Gloucestershire, a few miles east of Bristol.

In 1752, the failure of the harvest was immediately followed by a cattle plague which wiped out many of the local herds. The poor suffered greatly, and the Kingswood Colliers, already outcast, feared and despised, suffered more than most. Latimer, writing of a few years earlier, tells us that **"many hundreds of families were scattered over what had anciently been a royal forest, grovelling in wretched hovels, utterly uncared for by the half-dozen, 'Lords' who had usurped the land.**

A rumour swept through the Forest that wheat was to be exported from Bristol and this was the spark which lit smouldering unrest into open rebellion. In May 1753, the colliers, many hundred strong, marched on Bristol. Half-clothed, ragged, unkempt and dirty, their bodies still streaked with the black of the coal-pits, but stirred by positive action, they went seeking redress for their plight. Ravaged by hunger, they attempted to fill their empty bellies with the sprigs of *green hawthorn which grew along the way. This, with bitter irony, they called 'Bread and Cheese.''**

---

*As a child, after Sunday School and dressed uncomfortably in best clothes, with my parents and brother, I always took a Sunday walk along the then leafy lanes of Kingswood. When my brother and I became hungry, as children always will, my father, Jack Pillinger, would tell us to eat some "Bread and Cheese," pointing to the hawthorns. When questioned, Dad admitted he did not know the reason he called it so, except that his father had called it that. When I attempted this story and read of the colliers eating the hawthorns, I recalled the "Bread and Cheese" of my youth. It is interesting to know of an instance of Folk Memory, preserved in this way, handed down from father to son for a period of more than two hundred years.

[I have eaten much "bread and cheese" from the hawthorn tree as a youth—AUTHOR]

A week of rioting then ensued, which caused a Special Constabulary to be formed, and finally when this failed, a unit of the Scots Greys was summoned to the fray. These facts are dealt with in general in all the printed Bristol Histories, but none of the accounts name any of the colliers themselves. These savage and desperate men were "my people" and I set about to find who they were.

Felix Farley's Journal, dated May 26th 1753 gives a very detailed account of the week's rioting, culminating in the arrival of the army, who "firing a few pieces among them put them into such confusion they ran divers ways in order to make their escape." There follows a list of those taken and committed to Newgate. [Prison]

Job Phipps	Francis Muntin	Benj Crew
John Sibley	------ Muntin	George Gay
Edw Stanley	John Kendall	Nathaniel Crew
Geo Owler	Anthony Sawley	John Legg
Wm Pater	Rich Holloway	Thomas Maggs
Elias Emoty	Jacob Sage	Samuel Bonner
Charles Jones	Wm Weekes	and four more
Samuel Iles	Wm Woodward	(un-named)
Francis Iles	Emanuel Evans	
Robert Randall	Wm Young	

There is an added report: "The slain are Jonathon Crew, James Bryan and ------ Gunning whose bodies are carried to St. Peter's Hospital and Wm Fudge who was killed without Lawford's Gate."

The newspaper of May 31st 1753 records that the colliers in Newgate petitioned the Mayor that surgeons should be sent to dress their wounds. He was pleased to grant this request - but that such a plea should have been necessary seems shocking in *our own time. Certain well disposed citizens made a collection, and a **"Great Deal of Provision"** was sent outside the walls and into the Forest, where there were **"upwards of fifty wounded, some of them likely to lose their limbs."** With what hope of recovery one wonders? Three inquests at least are known on the bodies of colliers who died of their wounds. It is interesting that at these inquests verdicts of **"wilful murder"** were given by Edward West, county court coroner, against John Brickdale, woollen draper and Michale Miller, jeweller, presumably special constables. These verdicts were quashed on Government intervention and Brickdale and his companion were granted a general pardon.*

*Meanwhile, the hunt for the ring-leaders of the riot was gathering pace. August 4th 1753: **"His Majesty has ordered a reward of two hundred pounds to be paid to any persons who shall apprehend Sampson Phipps, one of the persons concerned in the Late Riot here, and one hundred pounds for apprehending either Samuel Britten, John Woody, otherwise Wordy, John Summers and Hezekiah Hunt likewise."** To the starving colliers it must have seemed, literally, a King's Ransom. It is to Kingswood's eternal credit that despite such an overwhelming inducement, none of the above named were ever given up.*

MINING

*On August 9th, the following incident is reported, amusing perhaps, but not to the man concerned. **"Sunday last about one o'clock after noon, one Iles, a collier, one of the person's concerned in the late riot here made an attempt to escape in Women's clothes. He passed the door but had not gone many yards further e're he was discovered and conducted safe to his lodgings."***

On September 5th began the special Tribunal set up to try the rioters. In their absence, two bills for High Treason were found against Sampson Phipps, the younger, and Samuel Britten. Then Sir Sidney Stafford Smythe, Sir Richard Adams and the Mayor and Aldermen of the City began to deal with the smaller fry.

It is clear that there was considerable sympathy in Bristol for the men in the dock. Against 21 of the original thirty no-one could be found who was prepared to give evidence, and these

were set free. Of the ^remaining nine, Samuel Bonner, a
weaver, was dealt with leniently on account of his youth. No
age is given for him, but it can be safely assumed that he was a
mere child. He was sentenced to remain in prison for a further
six months and to pay a fine of thirteen shillings and
fourpence, to continue in prison until the fine be paid and to
enter into a Recognizance for his good behaviour for three
years, himself in £ 40 and his sureties in £ 20.

The rest, George Olds, Francis Muntin, Robert Holloway,
William Young, Benjamin Crew, Nathaniel Crew, William
Jefferies and John Paviour were all found guilty. There were
sentenced to two years imprisonment each, fined 13/4d with
the same provisos as Bonner. The Magistrates probably
congratulated themselves on their Christian magnanimity
and, if the sentences seem light, it must be remembered that
with the conditions prevailing in prison at the time, with Gaol
Fever, Small Pox and Starvation a constant hazard and the
heaviness of the fines and sureties on men stricken with un-
believable poverty, with no hope of payment, the penalties
imposed amounted to a virtual death sentence.

Shuffling in their leg irons, the prisoners made to leave the
dock, when Paviour and Jefferies were summoned back to
face another charge. There were indicted for feloniously
stealing a Hogshead of Sugar out of the ship "The Lamb"
bound for Dublin, which the rioters had boarded on the first
day of the affair, but "not in their Hurry examined so
particularly the contents of the Hogshead so as to be sure it
was Sugar" and the Bench must have groaned aloud in unison
disbelief that such a simple check had been overlooked; they
were acquitted on this count. They could have hanged; no
doubt they joined their fellows with some relief.

The dank, dripping walls of Newgate closed around the
Kingswood men and we do not hear of them again until
December 22nd when they thanked certain kind people, no
doubt moved by the festive season, for a donation of 6d
apiece. No further largesse seemed forthcoming however, and
in March the following year, the prisoners advertised their
plight:

"The Poor Unhappy Colliers now under confinement in
Newgate return thanks to their worthy Benefactors for what
relief they have already received and having nothing but Gaol
Allowance to subsist humbly hope that some other Well-
disposed Christians will take in consideration their deplorable
condition for whom they will ever be in duty bound to pray."

There is no evidence that this pathetic appeal brought forth
any response. It is a far cry from the fire in the blood when

the march on Bristol had begun almost a year before. Unfortunately, no records remain to show whether they were ever released from prison. Unable to pay their fines and wracked with disease it is probable they were forgotten except by the sweethearts, wives, mothers and children who sorrowed and despaired without them in the forest. [Patricia Lindegaard, "The Colliers' Tale--A Bristol Incident of 1753," *Journal of the Bristol and Avon Family History Society,* Spring 1978]

Some of your ancestors may have been military men. Military life was very rough. A glance at the regimental discharge for this and the nineteenth centuries tells a tragic story. Here are thousands of young men less than thirty years of age being discharged because of rheumatism--men who had to be on duty in wet clothes, had to sleep in wet clothes, and consequently were physically impaired before they had really started to live.

There are heroes on both sides of any military confrontation. This was well illustrated when the British troops were engaged in the American War of Independence. Elizabeth Hopkins, wife of a sergeant in the 104th, proved herself a worthy wife for a soldier in the American War of Independence. After being wounded in the left leg in a naval action in which she was helping to serve the guns, she contrived the escape of her husband (who had been captured by the enemy), provided him and twenty-two deserters who accompanied him with arms and ammunition, and led them back to Philadelphia despite pursuit by a body of dragoons. One of these, who attacked and wounded her in the arm, she shot, and rode back on his horse in triumph. Later she showed great gallantry in the siege of Pensacola, where she was captured with the rest of the garrison after helping to serve in the batteries and using strips of her clothing as wadding for the guns. Released on parole, she was shipwrecked while "in a certain condition," rescued, and delivered of triplets--an experience which could have been no novel one to her, for her children numbered twenty-two all told, of whom eleven survived. She seems to have been a truly Spartan mother, for, after seeing two of her sons and one son-in-law killed before her eyes at Fort Erie, she "called her other children round her, made them an animated speech charging them to be revenged on the Yankees for their loss, and cheered them into action."

A Foot Soldier. Dress and equipment, 1759. Note the variety of Weapons.

Your ancestor may have served in the navy, though not necessarily by choice. From the fourteenth century right through to the nineteenth, your male ancestors, especially those living near the coast, were in danger of suddenly being whisked off to sea by a press gang. This was perfectly within the law, the press gang being in the charge of a commissioned officer of the Royal Navy. It was a quick though sometimes brutal method of completing a ship's company before it sailed. Several years later, your ancestor might have made his way home to find his bride remarried. (Communications were not like they are today.)

A British Infantryman, 1745.

A Press Gang Seizing a Young Man for Service in the Navy.
(Based on print in Oxford Magazine, 1770.)

English sailor wearing trousers, 1737.

Discipline on board ship had to be severe. If your ancestor got into trouble, he might be given a number of lashes with a cat-o'-nine-tails. Forty-five lashes was considered sufficient to kill a person of average stamina.

Poor John Wilson, in 1779, had deserted, been caught, and received fifty lashes. Several days later the crews of several nearby navy ships were gathered together, and they witnessed the same John Wilson given 450 lashes, clearly a death sentence and a stern lesson to the crews of the assembled ships.

Joseph Rooke could have written quite an exciting personal history. There are thousands of such examples, many of them connected to those of you who boast English ancestry.

Concerning Joseph Rooke, an old sailor, born in New York, taken up as a vagabond, 1743.

The examination of Joseph Rooke a vagabond taken upon oath 15 June 1743 before me John Pickering Esq., one of his Majesty's Justices.

This examinant saith that he was born in the City of New

York in America, and when he was about the age of twenty two years he was pressed on board the Britania Man of War and stayed on board about five months, and afterwards went on board the Triumph Man of War and stayed on board that ship about eleven months, and afterwards he went on board the Grafton man of war and stay'd in that ship about six years and until she was taken prisoner by the French, and after he got into England from France, he went on board the Flamborough man of war and stayed there about three years and a half, and some time afterwards he was pressed from on board a merchant ship on board the Grafton man of war and stay'd in the Grafton about four months in which said ship this examinant lost his left arm by a connon ball, after which he was admitted a pentioner from the Chest at Chatham, and he does not know that he hath done any act matter or thing whatsoever to gain him any other legal settlement since his birth . . . [Cheshire Quarter Sessions Record, I, 218]

A Naval Seaman early 18th century. Most sailors were pressed into the Service.

Many of your ancestors were slave owners, while others may have tried to improve the condition of slaves, even by freeing them. Such a person was Granville Sharp, born in 1738, the son of a clergyman and grandson of the archbishop of York. After much effort, he established in Sierra Leone a colony for freed slaves from British colonies and named it Freetown. Truly, an ancestor to be proud of.

In the eighteenth century, schools were still not numerous and for the "fortunate few." Following are some of the statutes drawn up for the establishment of Robert Boyle's Free School at Bolton Abbey, Yorkshire, 1701.

Statute 3d. The Mr shall . . . take speciall care of the Scholars not only in the School, that they do diligently Apply themselves to their Books . . . but also out of the School, whereby their . . . recreations may be so Regulated, that no Swearing, Cursing, Lying, or any rude Immodest or irreverent behaviour . . . be used . . . neither shall he suffer any of his scholars (If he can possiblly prevent it) to Converse with Idle, Loose and prophane persons . . .

Statute 5th. The Mr or Usher shall not for any offence wtsoever Correct any Boy upon any part of the head, But (upon their demerits) shall smite or clap them with the flat side of a plaine wooden Ferula, or . . . with a rod upon one hand, or whip them with a small birch rod upon the Buttocks, as the fault deserves, And If such correction be found ineffectuall then the Master shall order the Criminall name and fault to be noted down in a bill called the blackbill . . . to Restraine them from all liberty of playing . . . they shall be confined to their books . . . and be forced by a more sever whiping (If they thn neglect) to performe all such tasks as the Mr or Usher shall enjoyn them which punishment shall be continued till they reform. . .

Statute 6th. None shall be received into the sd School who have scald heads, or are not perfectly recovered from the small pox, Meazels, or Feavers, or have upon them any Ulcerous or Soars, or any loathsome contagions or Infectious distempers wtsoever but upon the first discovery they shall be immeadiatly sent to their friends to be perfectly cured . . . also all such Scholars as the Mr shall perceive to be Naturally very dull, and upon one or two years tryall, are found utterly incapable of Learning shall (wth the Consent of the Trustees for the sd School . . .) be returned to their Parents, or Guardians wthout further trouble to the sd School, and all such wicked . . . and Obstinate scholars as . . . refuse to observe . . . the statues . . . shall . . . be Expelled . . . and the reason of it . . . Registred in a Book

Statute 10th. The Mr and Usher shall duely resort to the Parish Church every Sunday, Holy-day and other days of Publick humiliation & thanksgiving . . . and Oblige . . . all the Scholars to be present there . . . And that they behave . . . wth humility and Reverence Expressing the Devotion of their Souls by the bodily postures of Kneeling, standing, or otherwise as the order of service Requires . . . And once every week the Mr and Usher shall teach Instruct . . . the Church Catechism to the Schollars . . .

Statute 11th. The School shall open every morning at Seaven a clock all the Year round, wth . . . prayers and Imeadiatly after . . . the Mr shall begin . . . to teach till Eleven . . . And (. . . after two hours Intermission he shall . . . continue till the Evening prayers at five a Clock . . .) [From *Yorkshire Schools and Schooldays,* paper no. 14, Jan 1976, University of Leeds Institute of Education]

In 1761 the first canal was cut and before the end of the nineteenth century, thousands of miles of canal joined navigable rivers to make commercial transportation by barge a very economical method. Thus we find some of our ancestors spending their lives in the boats on the inland waterways. They were commonly called 'watermen' and 'bargees'.

Their children, your ancestors, would be baptized when convenient, if at all, when the barge was tied up near some parish churches. The children received the same education that their working-class parents received--from the school of hard knocks or whatever their parents could teach them. They probably spent many hours reading the Holy Bible or having it read to them during the long winter nights. An example of writing a family history of a waterman family appears in the final chapter.

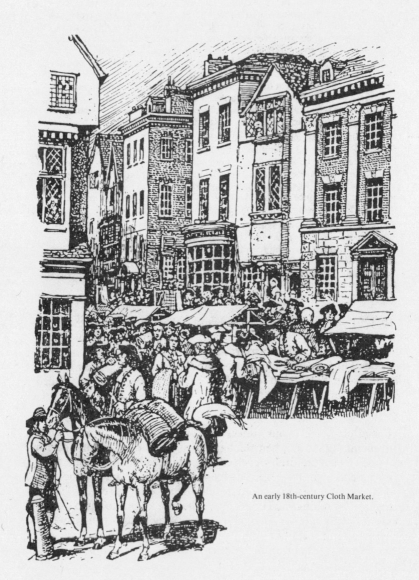

An early 18th-century Cloth Market.

The parish church of Holy Trinity at Pleshey

THE NINETEENTH CENTURY

HISTORICAL	RELIGIOUS	RECORD-KEEPING	SOCIAL, ECONOMICAL
		1800 Earliest date in known Bible Christian registers.	1801 First steam boat and steam carriage. First population census taken, but not of any genealogical value.
			1802 First London sewer.
1803 Napoleon planned to conquer Europe and invade England.			1804 Trevithick's first railroad locomotive.
1805 Naval victory at Trafalgar.		1806 Earliest date in known Primitive Methodist registers.	
1807 Population of England and Wales reached 11 million.			1807 Abolition of the slave trade.
1808 British army in Portugal.			
1809 British army at Antwerp (Belgium).	1810 Bible Christians denomination formed by schism in Wesleyan Methodists.		
	1810-12 Primitive Methodists formed after expulsion from Wesleyan Connexion.		
1812-13 French armies driven out of Spain, Portugal, and Germany.		1813 New type of parish register books consisting of ruled and numbered pages, introduced.	
1812-14 American War of 1812 against England and Canada.		1814 Act of burial in woolen repealed.	1814 Stephenson's first steam engine. Great distress through depression of trade due to war.
1815 Battle of Waterloo. Napoleon defeated.			1819 Corn laws enacted which impoverished the poor. Riots in connection with social reforms.
1820 GEORGE IV (1820-30).			1821 Steamboats plied English Channel.

HISTORICAL	RELIGIOUS	RECORD-KEEPING	SOCIAL, ECONOMICAL
		1823 New laws concerning marriage by license passed.	
1830 WILLIAM IV (1830-37).	1829 Catholic Emancipation Act; triumph of religious toleration.	1829 Earliest known registers of the Irvingite or Catholic Apostolic group.	1829 First paid police.
		1831 A list of all parish registers before 1813 compiled.	1830 Opening of first railways.
			1833 Trade unionism gained strength.
		1835 Earliest known date in Universalist church registers.	1833-35 Slaves in British colonies emancipated.
1837 VICTORIA (1837-1902).		1837 New law concerning the civil registration of births, marriages, and deaths enforced from 1 July.	
			1839 First bicycle.
		1841 The first population census of value to genealogists taken.	1842 Penny postage introduced. Royal Commission of Mines found that women pulled the coal trucks on hands and feet and children of five worked alone in the darkness. Such practices forbidden by law.
			1846 Irish potato famine.
			1847 Ten Hour Act limited women and children to ten hours of work a day in textile factories.
		1851 The population census improved; information of great value to genealogists added.	1851 Population reached 27,600,000.

THE NINETEENTH CENTURY

HISTORICAL	RELIGIOUS	RECORD-KEEPING	SOCIAL, ECONOMICAL
1854-56 The Crimean War.		1858 Probate courts taken out of ecclesiastical jurisdiction.	1858 Jews admitted to Parliament.
1861-65 American Civil War.			1861-65 Lancashire cotton trade distressed due to American Civil War.
			1870 Married Women's Property Acts passed protecting their use and disposal of their own property.
		1872 Penalties enforced for failing to register births, marriages, or deaths.	
1879 Zulu War. 1899 South Africa (Boer) War.			

Chapter 4

THE NINETEENTH CENTURY

Houseless near a thousand homes,
And near a thousand tables pine for want of food.
Oh shame that bread should be so dear,
And human lives so cheap

This was a century of great upheavals in English society. With the industrial movement now in full swing, the population was able to move more rapidly, there were adjustments in employment and great unemployment and much misery among the working people.

The unemployment was a prime factor in a great exodus to America and the colonies. The adjoining table shows emigration from the British Isles between 1815 and 1900. Most of the emigrants went to the United States and Canada.

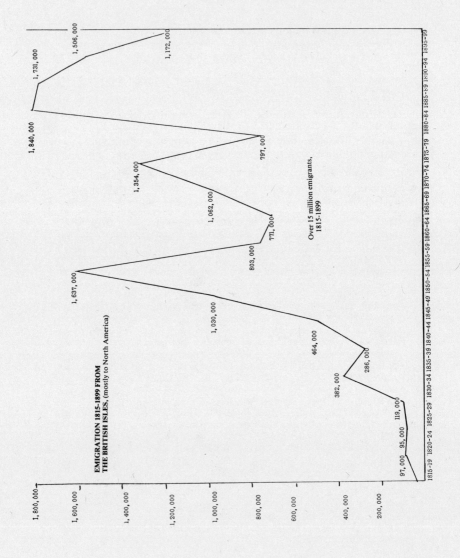

EMIGRATION 1815-1899 FROM
THE BRITISH ISLES, (mostly to North America)

Over 15 million emigrants,
1815-1899

The only truly voluntary exodus of this time was that of those who had embraced the Mormon faith from 1837 onwards and who eventually assisted in the colonizing of the western United States. But most emigrants left for economic reasons.

William Hall, a small farmer in England, gave these reasons for leaving England in 1821: (1) to more readily provide for his large family; (2) to escape oppression, misery, hypocrisy, and tyranny; (3) to seek civil and religious liberty in America; (4) to escape a hopeless amelioration since there was no prospect of amelioration in England; and (5) to point out the same road to distressed friends and relatives. (See Howard B. Furer, *The British in America, 1578-1970* [Oceana Publications, 1972])

The continual failure of the potato crop in Ireland caused many Irish to move to England and even more to America and other countries. In the 1822 famine, three million were reduced to starvation levels in Ireland. In spite of millions of pounds' worth of food exported from England to Ireland, conditions in the 1830s described by a contemporary reviewer as follows:

Those who have never travelled in Ireland can form but a very imperfect idea of the distress that generally pervades that unhappy country. Often have I seen in one miserable, nearly unroofed dwelling, with scarcely a window remaining, from ten to twelve, **and in some instances more,** families, penned up together, with not an article of household furniture save the shattered remains of an old oak table, or a solitary chair without a back, or a broken stool. And for culinary utensils an iron pot not unfrequently serves the three-fold purposes of tea kettle, **if they are able to raise the tea,** a pot to boil the potatoes in, or stirabout, **meat they have none,** and a vessel to wash the tattered remains of their wretched garments in; these, with **perhaps** a broken cup and saucer, make up the sum of the whole of their moveable effects. In every street and alley are to be seen groups of human beings in a state of half nudity; women with their almost lifeless infants struggling to obtain a portion of the scanty nutriment from their exhausted mothers, while their reckless and infuriated father wander the streets, lost to all hope, and maddened with hunger and despair. Nay, I have frequently seen women with the lifeless bodies of their infant children in their arms, prowling from street to street, and begging from the casual passengers the means of depositing the remains of their departed offspring in the grave!

Around the 1830s however, conditions were not much better in England. They were so bad in fact, that many English families were encouraged, and even financially assisted, to emigrate. The United States, Canada, Australia, New Zealand, and South Africa were all recipients of these poor families.

The local newspaper for Bury St. Edmunds, Suffolk, for 30 April 1830 reads in part:

Seventy-eight men, women and children from Diss, Palgrave and Wortham and fifty-eight from Winfarthing and Shelfhanger passed through Bury in stage waggons on the way to London to take shipping for America. They were in high spirits.

A Country Waggon for carrying Goods and Passengers before the days of Railways.
(*Based on a contemporary print,* circa 1820.)

Expenses were paid by varous emigration societies or by the Poor Law Act of 1834. In this area, Suffolk, it cost over £13 per year to support a family that had no employment. It cost about £60 to transport the family to America. If the family were to be unemployed for several years, as was sometimes likely, then the parish realized a savings and eased the unemployment burden by helping the family emigrate (See Pursehouse, *Waveney Valley Studies*)

In 1830, 56,907 persons emigrated from the British Isles. This number fluctuated but gradually increased so that by 1850, 280,000 emigrated. Around 80 percent of these-consistently, year by year went to the United States. By the turn of the century, however, this percentage had declined, and emigration to the colonies greatly increased.

Besides those who left for economic and religious reasons, there were others who were deported for social reasons. Most of them went to Australia. However, transportation of so-called criminals to Australia varied just as much with the need for settlers as with the seriousness of the crimes. Some persons were exported for small crimes and others only placed in prison for similar or more serious crimes:

From a Calendar of Prisoners at Surrey Quarter Sessions, 1848.

Henry Eldridge (Aged 18, can neither read nor write). Committed the 8th of February by G. P. Elliott, esq., charged on the oaths of Frederick France and others, with feloniously stealing, at Lambeth, Two coats, and other articles, his property. Transported seven years.

The so-called criminal on his way to Australia had an awful time. His situation when he landed was no better and with the same punishment year after year, many committed suicide. Others escaped and died of starvation. An excellent description of the life of a convict is vividly portrayed in *For the Term of His Natural Life* by Marcus Clarke (Oxford University Press, 1952). Here is a brief description of life on the convict ship taken from that book:

> The prison was about fifty feet long and fifty feet wide, and ran the full height of the 'tween decks, viz., about five feet ten inches high. The barricade was loop-holed here and there, and the planks were in some places wide enough to admit a musket barrel. On the aft side, next the soldiers' berths, was a trap door, like the stoke-hole of a furnace. At first sight, this appeared to be contrived for the humane purpose of ventilation, but a second glance dispelled this weak conclusion. The opening was just large enough to admit the muzzle of a small howitzer, secured on the deck below. In case of a mutiny, the soldiers could sweep the prison from end to end with grape shot. Such fresh air as there was, filtered through the loop holes, and came, in somewhat larger quantity, through a wind-sail passed into the prison from the hatchway. But the wind-sail being necessarily at one end only of the place, the air it brought was pretty well absorbed by the twenty or thirty lucky fellows near it, and the other hundred and fifty did not come so well off. The scuttles were open, certainly, but as the row of bunks had been built against them, the air *they* brought was the peculiar property of such men as occupied the berths into which they penetrated. These berths were twenty-eight in number, each containing six men. They ran in a double tier round three sides of the prison, twenty at each side, and eight affixed to that portion of the forward barricade opposite the door. Each berth was presumed to be five feet six inches square, but the necessities of stowage had deprived them of six inches, and even under that pressure twelve men were compelled to sleep on the deck. Pine did not exaggerate when he spoke of the custom of overcrowding convict ships; and he was entitled to half a guinea for every man he delivered alive at Hobart Town, he had some reason to complain . . . .

> Old men, young men, and boys, stalwart burglars and highway robbers, slept side by side with wizened pickpockets or cunning-featured area-sneaks. The forger occupied the same berth with the bodysnatcher. The man of education learned strange secrets of house-breakers' craft, and the vulgar ruffian of St. Giles took lessons of self control from the keener intellect of the professional swindler. The fraudulent clerk and flash 'cracksman' interchanged experiences. The smuggler's stories of lucky ventures and successful runs were capped by the footpad's reminiscences of foggy nights and stolen watches. The poacher, grimly thinking of his sick wife and orphaned children, would start as the night-house ruffian clapped him on the shoulder and bade him, with a curse, to take good heart and 'be a man.' The fast shopboy, whose love of fine company and high living had brought him to this pass, had shaken off the first shame that was on him, and listened eagerly to the narratives of successful vice that fell so glibly from the lips of his older companions. To be transported seemed no such uncommon fate. The old fellows laughed, and wagged their grey heads with all the glee of past experience, and listening youth longed for the time when it might do likewise. Society was the common foe, and magistrates, jailers, and parsons, were the natural prey of all noteworthy mankind. Only fools were honest, only cowards kissed the rod, and failed to meditate revenge on that world of respectability which had wronged them. Each new comer was one more recruit to the ranks of ruffianism, and not a man penned in that reeking den of infamy but became a sworn hater of law, order, and 'free-men.'' What he

might have been before mattered not. He was now a prisoner, and thrust into a suffocating barracoon, herded with the foulest of mankind, with all imaginable depths of blasphemy and indecency sounded hourly in his sight and hearing—he lost his self-respect, and became what his jailers took him to be—a wild beast to be locked under bolts and bars, lest he should break out and tear them.

While many were emigrating to foreign lands, many Scottish and Irish settled in England. The following is an example of conditions in Scotland that caused Scots, particularly from the Highlands, to go abroad or to go south to England:

We were asked by a person almost starving to go into a house. We there found on one side of the fire a very old man, apparently dying; on the other side a young man of about eighteen, with a child on his knee, whose mother had just died and been buried; and evidently both that young man and the child were suffering from want. . . We went upstairs, and under some rags we found another young man, the widower, and turning down the rags, which he was unable to remove himself, we found another man who was dying, and who did die in the course of the day. I have no doubt that the whole family were actually starving at the time. [Evidence given before a committee of investigation]

Thus we see in this century a changing England: an oversupply of unskilled labor; crop failure; and movement of poor Scots, Irish and Welsh to England, while large numbers of English were going abroad.

These great upheavals were in part, of course, a result of the Industrial Revolution, which had begun in the previous century. The disruptive effects of this revolution on life in the first half of the nineteenth century are typified in the following description from Charles Dickens's *Dombey & Son:*

The first shock of a great earthquake had rent the whole neighbourhood to its centre. Traces of its course were visible on every side. Houses were knocked down; streets broken through and stopped; deep pits and trenches dug in the ground; enormous heaps of earth and clay thrown up; buildings that were undermined and shaking, propped by great beams of wood. Here, a chaos of carts, overthrown and jumbled together, lay topsy-turvy at the bottom of a steep unnatural hill; there, confused treasures of iron soaked and rusted in something that had become a pond.

This is not a description of aerial bombardment but simply a description of the preparation for the railroad in Camden Town, London, in 1836.

The physical chaos Dickens describes had its social counterpart in the early nineteenth century. This social disorder naturally led to oppressive measures:

5 THE "PETERLOO MASSACRE" MANCHESTER, 1819 (From an old print.)

The land of Magna Charta was for nearly a generation controlled by a reactionary government which could by no stretch of the imagination be termed democratic. Habeas Corpus and the freedom of speech and public meeting were almost entirely suppressed; the press was either throttled or gagged; while all but the most eminent Whigs were liable to intensive persecution in a day when statements like Bishop Horsley's -- that he did not know what the mass of the people of any country had to do with the laws except to obey them -- went almost unchallenged.

Methods of keeping order obviously had to change. For hundreds of years the parish constable had kept the peace. This was a yearly office, a voluntary assignment. Men were drawn from the inhabitants of the parish and appointed by the Justices of the Peace for the county.

A "Peeler," or member sf the Metropolitan Police Force founded by Sir Robert Peel, 1829.

BOBBY OR "PEELER" 1829.

As the population grew, the need arose for a stronger and more permanent peace-keeping force. Established by Robert Peel, they were first known as **Peelers** and later as **Bobbies, Bobby** or **Bob** being a dimunitive of **Robert.**

One of Sir Robert Peel's New Police, 1829. They wore swallow-tailed, dark blue coats, white trousers and a leather tall hat.

However, our ancestors resisted change just as much as we do today. The resistance to the new police force is shown in the following:

> 1841. To the Chairman and Magistrates of the County of Gloucester in Quarter Sessions Assembled.
>
> The Petition of the Undersigned Inhabitants of the Parish of Compton Greenfield in the County of Gloucester Humbly Sheweth
>
> That your Petitioners first heard with surprise of the Establishment of a County Police, a Measure which they consider not only as exceedingly expensive but absolutely unncessary and useless. That the peaceful habits of our Population require no such watch upon their actions nor any such check upon their innocent amusements; and when any mistrust or disturbance has arisen among them a single Admonition from their Masters and Employers has always been found a sufficient corrective without the aid of a Constable. . .
>
> *Gloucestershire Quarter Sessions Archives*

Not only has the nature of peace-keeping forces changed over the centuries, but so has the nature of the laws they enforce. In our ancestors' days, the Sabbath day was not to be trifled with, as evidenced by the following conviction at Macclesfield (Cheshire) assizes, 12 August 1823:

> 12 August 1823 Olive Wood convicted of working her mangle on the Lord's Day. Fined 5/- and expenses.

Leaving your work before the duly appointed hour was serious business as evidenced at the same assizes:

> 30 August 1823 Powell and Sons against Mary Kirkham for leaving her work. Paid expenses and returned.

Although these practices are still wrong, hardly anyone today would be convicted for them.

A Parish Beadle removing homeless children to the Workhouse.
(Based on Wilkie's picture, circa 1822.)

The medicine administered to bad boys might sometimes be applied today.

From the same record:

> 31 May 1824 James Dernily a very bad youth who ran away from his master and shapes for ruin. Given him a good whipping and sent home.

Although people were still imprisoned for what we now consider petty offenses, the conditions in prison were changing.

The prisons of the previous century had been of a deplorable nature. There had been insufficient food and clothing, water, ventilations, and sanitation. The prisoners had been crowded together, without regard to crime or sex. After many campaigns, spread over many years, great improvements were made so that by the 1830s

NEWGATE PRISON, 1782-1904.

one prisoner wrote:

> I cannot take my walks abroad, I'm under lock and key;
> And much the public I applaud, for all their care of me.
> Not more than others I deserve, in fact much less than more;
> Yet I have food while others starve, or beg from door to door.
> The honest pauper in the street half naked I behold;
> While I am clad from head to feet and covered from the cold.
> Thousands there are who scarce can tell where they may lay their head;
> But I've a warm bed and well air'd cell, a bath, good books, good bed.
> While they are fed on workhouse fare, and grudged their scanty food;
> Three times a day my meals I get, sufficient, wholesome, good.
> Then to the British public health, who all our care relieves
> And while they treat us as they do, they'll never want for thieves.
>
> [*Bulletin of the Institute of Historical Research*, May 1978]

However, as we have noted there was still severe punishment for very minor crimes. Note these interesting examples from records in the record office at Aylesbury, Buckinghamshire:

Register number: 5826
Occupation: field worker
Age: 64
Marital status: widow
Crime: stole shawl
Sentence: 1 month hard labour

Register number: 5898
Occupation: clerk
Age: 22
Marital status: ?
Crime: stole money
Sentence: 9 months hard labour
and 2 years police
supervision

Register number: 5488
Occupation: domestic servant
Age: 16
Marital status: ?
Crime: stole a pair of shoes
Sentence: 1 month hard labour

Register number: 5539
Occupation: servant
Age: 20
Marital status: single
Crime: stole money
Sentence: 3 months hard labour

Register number: 5433
Occupation: groom
Age: 30
Marital status: single
Crime: stole a pair of boots
Sentence: 42 days hard labour

Register number: 5891
Occupation: hawker
Age: 79
Marital status: widow
Crime: stole 4 lbs. starch
Sentence: 7 days hard labour

Register number: 5199
Occupation: housekeeper
Age: 40
Marital status: married
Crime: stole preserved ginger
Sentence: 14 days hard labour

Register number: 5198
Occupation: domestic servant
Age: 16
Marital status: ?
Crime: stole money from master
Sentence: 1 month hard labour

Register number: 4295
Occupation: navvy
Age: 26
Marital status: single
Crime: stole a shirt
Sentence: 21 days hard labour

Register number: 5666
Occupation: hawker
Age: 43
Marital status: widower
Crime: stole purse and money
Sentence: 4 months hard labour

Register number: 5504
Occupation: domestic servant
Age: 20
Marital status: single
Crime: stole a pair of boots
Sentence: 6 weeks hard labour

Register number: 5489
Occupation: housekeeper
Age: 51
Marital status: married, 8 children
Crime: stole wood
Sentence: 10 days hard labour

As bad as it was to be sent to prison, for some it was only slightly worse than being sent to the workhouse. In fact, I can remember as a young boy, the stigma that went with sending older relatives to the workhouse.

In 1835 the country was divided into Poor Law Unions. Groups of parishes within the unions sent their sick, their destitute, their unwed mothers, and their aged to the new workhouses.

A little earlier, Crabbe had described the workhouse thusly:

Their's is yon house that holds the Parish-Poor,
Whose walls of mud scarce bear the broken door;
There, where the putrid vapours, flagging, play,
And the dull wheel hums doleful through the day;
There Children dwell who know no Parent's care;
Parents, who know no Children's love, dwell there!
Heart-broken Matrons on their joyless bed,
Forsaken Wives and Mothers never wed;
Dejected Widows with unheeded tears,
And crippled Age with more than childhood fears;
The Lame, the Blind, and far the happiest they!
The moping Idiot and the Madman gay.
Here, too, the Sick their final doom receive,
Here brought, amid the scenes of grief, to grieve,
Where the loud groans from some sad chamber flow,
Mixt with the clamours of the crowd below;
Here sorrowing they each their kindred sorrow scan,
And the cold charities of man to man:
Whose laws indeed for ruin'd Age provide,
And strong compulsion plucks the scrap from pride:
But still the scrap is brought with many a sigh,
And pride embitters what it can't deny.

[Quoted in Frank Smith, *The Lives and Times of Our English Ancestors*, Vol. 1. Logan: Everton Publishers, 1969, p. 157]

The following entry from a parish account book provides a glimpse at the daily routine of a typical workhouse of this century-the one located in the parish of Dovedale, Derbyshire. The main item is the death of Jane Slater, but why the snuff?

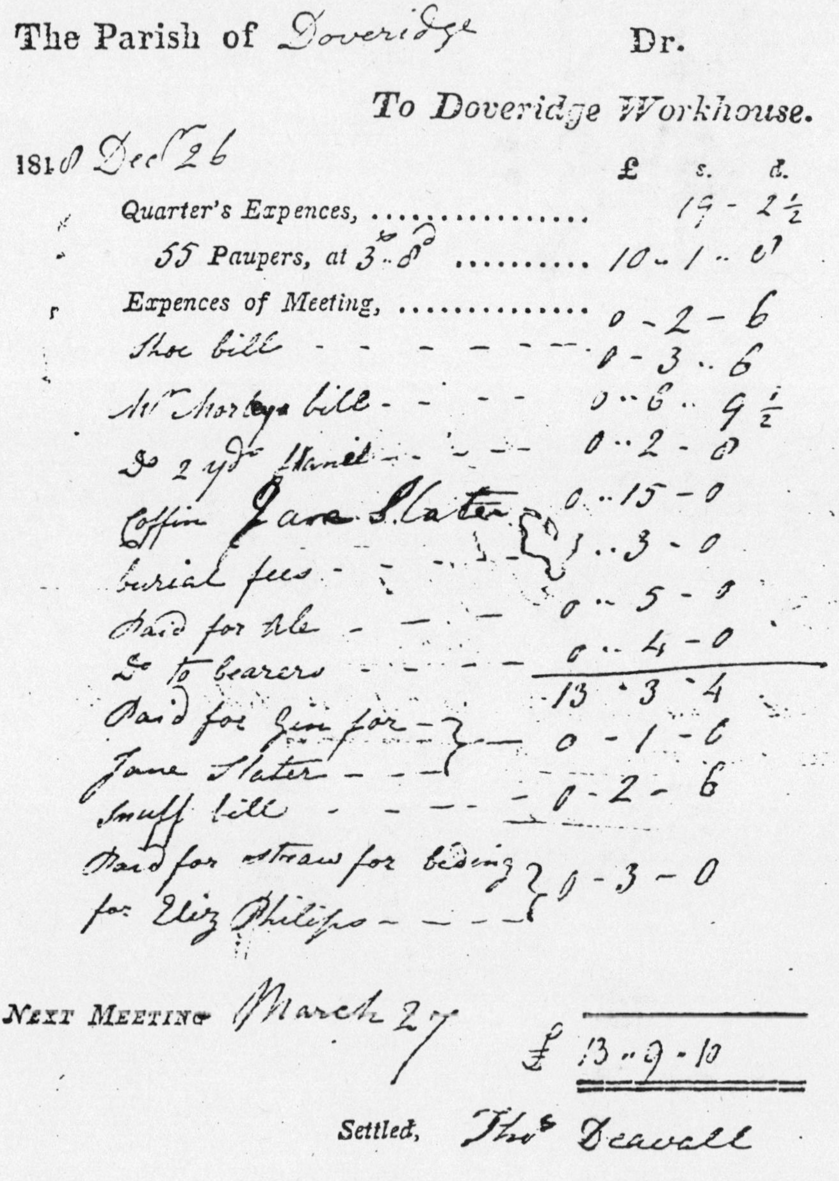

The Parish of *Doveridge*   Dr.

                              To *Doveridge Workhouse.*

1810 *Dec 26*   £   s.   d.

    Quarter's Expences, ...   *19 - 2½*
    55 Paupers, at *3..8* ....   *10 - 1 - 0*
    Expences of Meeting, ...   *0 - 2 - 6*
    Shoe bill - - - - - -   *0 - 3 - 6*
    Mr Morleys bill - - - -   *0 - 6 - 9½*
    Do 2 yds Flanel - - -   *0 - 2 - 0*
    Coffin Jane Slater   *0 - 15 - 0*
    burial fees - -   *1 - 3 - 0*
    Paid for ale - -   *0 - 5 - 0*
    Do to bearers - - -   *0 - 4 - 0*
                         13 - 3 - 4
    Paid for gin for   *0 - 1 - 6*
    Jane Slater - -
    Snuff bill - - - -   *0 - 2 - 6*
    Paid for straw for bedding   *0 - 3 - 0*
    for Eliz Philips - - -

NEXT MEETING March 27

                              £ *13 - 9 - 10*

                      Settled, *Thos Deavall*

This example of an appeal for extra allowances it taken from the records of the Titchfield (Hampshire) Poorhouse, 1 July 1835:

Name	Monthly	Daily		Remarks
James CLEVERLY	Monthly 2s.	Daily 1 pt. Ale		Usefully mends shoes, Decrepid and infirm.
William HARRIS	"	"		Trustworthy; cuts & has charge of the wood, runs errands.
James BONE	" 1s.	" Extra bread & cheese		Very useful & takes care of the garden & keeps it in order himself.
Emanuel GRIFFEN	" "	" 1pt. Ale		Attends to baking.
John Cullimore	" "	" " "		Very useful, takes care of the Oakum & assists in keeping the boys in order.
Mary KENT	" 2s.			Schoolmistress for the younger children.
Lydia CAREY	" 6 ozs. tea 1 oz. moist sugar			Very old, lame and blind.
Elizabeth PARSONS	" "			Very old, lame and much palsied.
Harriet BARNES	" "			Very useful, takes care of the old women, cooks, bakes, washes & generally useful.
Ann CHIDDLE	" "			Generally useful when wanting.

From the Hampshire Family Historian, 1977.

Earlier than this, some of the larger parishes had workhouses of their own. More often than not, these were poorly maintained, as the following item points out:

Edgmond Parish Workhouse, [1825]

A long and detailed account by Thomas Leeke, Esqre., of the disgraceful condition of this [workhouse], in which there were 20 persons, 9 of them children. The wet comes in everywhere, they have hardly any clothes or bedding, no superintendent lives in the house, no parish officer has been there for 3 weeks, "the whole establishment is shamefully neglected and inmates filthy, badly clothed, and the greater part idle. There is no work whatever going on in the house."

The Overseers were examined by the Court and detailed orders given to them as to the repairs to be done, and clothes and bedding to be provided, and that the acting Overseer for the time being must inspect it at least once a week. [Sir Offley Wakeman and R. Lloyd Kenyon, eds.,] *Shropshire County Records:* Orders of the Shropshire Quarter Sessions, 5 vols (n.p., n.d.) 3:248

Let's take a look inside a typical workhouse in 1851. In the large town of Birmingham there were four. The one we will look in is the one in the ecclesiastical district of St. Phillip.

Work House, Birmingham

On the night of 30 March 1851, when the census was taken, there were 19 workhouse officials and 382 inmates. To give an idea of the size of such an operation and the type of people required to run it here is a list of the officials as it appeared in the census returns:

NAMES AND SURNAMES	CONDI-TION	AGES M	AGES F	RANK, PROFESSION OR OCCUPATION	WHERE BORN OR IF BORN IN COUNTY
Passmore, Philip	Wid	45		Master of Workhouse	Wolfardisworthy, Devon
Cooper, Sarah	Wid		39	Matron	Chepstow, Monmouth,
Munro, Samuel	Mrd	39		Porter	Hillsborough, Down, Ireland
Munro, Arabella	Mrd		30	Nurse	Cavan, Ireland
Price, John	Mrd	45		Tramp Master	Birmingham, Warw.
Ford, Hannah Maria	Unmrd		39	Kitchen Maid	Windiscombe, Somerset
White, Edward	Unmrd	39		Cook	Birmingham, Warw.
Slack, Frederick	Mrd	33		Insane Keeper	Derby
Giles, Fanny	Wid		39	Nurse	Italy, British subject
Hill, Alfred	Unmrd	24		House Surgeon	Walsall, Staffs
Clarke, Francis	Mrd	56		Beadle	Birmingham, Warws
Rogers, Ann	Wid		59	Nurse	Linea Mill, Salop
Lownds, Margaret	Wid		58	Nurse	Devonport, Devon
Ware, William	Wid	62		Night Watch	Birmingham, Warws
Edwards, Ann	Mrd		27	Nurse	Shrewsbury, Shrops
Taylor, Elizabeth	Wid		39	Laundress	Carmarthen, Wales
Hemming, Sarah	Mrd		46	Nurse	Abbots Morton, Worc.
Anthony, Sarah	Unmrd		35	Night Nurse	Wenlock, Shrops
Knight, Ann	Wid		62	Tramp Mistress	Gt. Packington, Warw.

The list of inmates is too long to record here but some of the more interesting ones are listed below. Bear in mind that the out-of-work, the sick, the lame, the idiot, were all mixed together under the same roof with little or no attempt at segregation.

NAME	CONDI-TION	AGES	RANK, PROFES-SION OR OCCUPA-TION	WHERE BORN OR IF BORN IN COUNTY
Betty, Richard	U	30	No trade, idiot	Birmingham
Chadwick, Henry	U	14	No trade	Northampton
[How did he get in here with no relatives?]				
Davis, Michael	Wid	40	Button Turner	Gibralter
[This widower is presumably out of work and has no home or other support for his children listed below.]				
Davis, Fanny		8		Birmingham, Warw.
Davis, Benjamin		6		" "
Davis, Mary Ann		4		" "
Davis, Thomas		2		" "
Hughes, Joseph	Wid	93	Gun Finisher	Birmingham, Warw.
Vale, Ann	U	73	Servant, Epileptic	Ireland
Bellamy, Ann	Mrd	30	Domestic Servant	Birmingham, Warw.
[Where is her husband?]				
Bellamy James	son	6 months		" "
Riley, Emma	U	14	None	" "
White, Ann	U	9		" "
[Are these orphans?]				
Prees, Emma	U	21	None	" "
[An unwed mother]				
Prees, Joseph	son	4 months		" "
Child/John	U	1		Glasgow, Scotland
[No mother listed with this child]				

Note: U signified unmarried

Dividing the inmates into age groups, we find:

37 between ages 1 and 10	31 between ages 41 and 50
37 between ages 11 and 20	50 between ages 51 and 60
62 between ages 21 and 30	69 between ages 61 and 70
36 between ages 31 and 40	60 over age 70

The latter is an alarming figure, suggesting that a large number of older people were sent there by their families to slowly die.

Most of the male inmates of working age had occupations typical to the Birmingham area and so were presumably just unemployed and without a home. The majority of the women were described as domestic servants, again presumably out of employment. A few inmates were born in Ireland. Those able, performed some kind of work for the institution.

We can again draw on Eric Pursehouse's *Waveney Valley Studies*
for social conditions among the poor around the Diss, Norfolk
area, typical of the rest of the country:

Study the state of things in Diss as the Overseers of the Poor recorded
them, month by month, when receiving "Requests at The House" from a
constant stream of poor people, literally begging at the Workhouse door for
work, money, clothes, bedding, fuel or tools.

Such requests were considered each month by the churchwardens, overseers
and others of the Workhouse Committee in the committee room at "The
House". Three books of requests have survived, covering 1809-1819, and
containing nearly 8,000 requests, an average of about 70 per month.

Apart from those for work, they were mainly for money for rents, sickness or
unemployment, to repay debts or equip apprentices; for footwear, clothing,
and materials—shoes, highlows [a laced boot, ankle high], flannel shirts,
shifts, petticoats, breeches, coats, slops [a frock, overgarment, or breeches],
etc.; for bedding—mattresses, ticks, quilts, pickling, coverlets, blankets,
sheets; for "firing"; for tools; and for "miscellaneous requirements".

Here, to illustrate the widespread poverty of the period, is a selection of
requests just as the overseers recorded them—with the committee's decision
in brackets:

Money requests—Sam Sandy wants more weekly, being able to do but
littel (Not Granted); Robt. Parr want to be excused rates (He is to pay rates,
but to be paid for tolling the Bell on Thursday); Susan Shibly want releif
being afflicted with ye evil (10s); Jno. Elsey request small sum of money to
put his son apprentice to shoemaker (40s. if bound properly); Joseph
Norman want Releif till get better and peice of flanel to wear next him
(Granted); Jas. Cattermole a littel extra releif, being incapabel of work, wife
having ye ague (Enquire); John Nobel bad with a wind rupture, beg a truss
(Truss); Jno. Leather want a nurse for wife and midwife, being near her time,
and a trifel for ye child when born: 8 children oldest 16 (Enquire); John
Sterlin want 6d a week more, his wife being incapabel of dressing or
undressing herself (Granted); Sarah Thurlow want weekly pay with her illeg.
child by Sam Capes, he being absconded (1s. 6d.); Wid. Rudd request pay as
usuall, very littell outdoor work (Enquire); Sam Woodrd want assistance
towards discharging a debt 4£ (Not Granted).

For clothes and materials—Ed. Page want pair shoes and stockens, shirt,
hat, slop, and pr. trowsers, going to business (Part); Thos. Potter request pr.
of Buskens (Not Granted); John Everson, 2 shirts, pr. Highlows and slops
for boy (Part); Sarah Avis, a bed gouen (G.); Henry Batley want a few yards
clorth for 3 children, and bedding (G. materials); Mary Hines, clorth for
shift, under petticoat, and more weekly (Shift); Robt. Woodrd want clorth
Highlow for daughter afflicktid with ye evil in her ancle (G.); Girl Bond at
Mr. Pyms, being going to continue, with an outside coat, shift, and 2
Handkercheifs (Half of them).

For bedding—Mariah Midson want picklin for bed teck, having no work
(N.G.); Beck Howe—something to lay on (G.); Wid. Cornell—a sheet (seem
to be much wanted) (G); John Peak, a slop and blankets (Slop only); Geo.
Thurlow's wife want child Bed linen and shift, being near her time: 7 chn.
(Part G.); Charles Feak want a pr. sheets and coverlid, 7 chn. at home
(N.G.); Wm. Cattermole, Highlows and Bed Tick (G.).

For fuel and firing—Wid. Henley an undercoat and something for coal
(2s. for coal); Wid. Mills request to be allowed ye Turf money (G.); Jno.
Lock 8s. towards ¼ chaldron coal (G.) Note—"Chaldron" was 36
bushels); Wid. Algar 3s. to purchase some furze now clearing away on
Stuston Common, and shoes mended (G.); Rich. Crisp, littell for fireing and
Extra Releif, child being bad with Hooping Cough (5s.).

For tools and work—Thos. Potter want a spade (Give spade, take off 1s. week); Abr. Hall—a woll wheel (Enquire); Sam Woodrow—a shirt and a scuppett having lost his in ye pitts (Half); Abr. Scott want a Hook and Shirt (Hook); Jno. Lords wife want a Tow wheel for learning Boy, and mentel for herself (Wheel); Roper—a spinning wheel (Enquire); Jno. Sadd want assistance, having no employ, or Give him a horse to enabel him to be employed carting brick (Enquire).

Other requests—Jas. Dack beg assistance towards ye loss of a sow and pigs, as appear by his petition (10s.); Wm. Barber beg 2 days lost time for refusing to pound two asses when ordered by his Master, and a pr. shoes (N.G.); Francis Ready had ye misfortune to loose a poney, Beg a little assistance towards ye loss (1£); Wid. Rudd exceeding sorry for offending ye overseer, Hopes ye Committee will be so kind as to re-allow her 6d. weekly (N.G.). [pp. 37ⁿ 39]

Reference was made in chapter 2 to the freezing over of the River Thames, a very unusual occurrence. The river froze again in 1827 and it was so cold that oxen were roasted on the ice. Imagine the misery of poor people as they tried to keep warm.

It is not surprising to find that, in this century of change, the place of children in society also changed. In the 1830s, the rector of Shelfanger, Norfolk, kept a notebook and records that young boys were sent out into the fields all day shooing birds away. Their food consisted only of barley bread (wheat was too dear), and their daily allowance was usually all eaten by nine each morning. Under such circumstances, it is not surprising that some youths became juvenile delinquents. Of course juvenile delinquents had existed before, but it was in this century that special handling was first given them. It began, as did many other charitable things, on a voluntary basis by philanthropists. Two of the better known organizations were the Philanthropic Society's school at Redhill, Surrey, and Captain Breton's school at Hackney, Middlesex. They began as places of treatment and schooling for destitute children, but by 1854, because of the increase in juvenile crime, the government had to step in. By 1866 they had become industrial schools and reformatories.

In a study made in 1883, the secretary of the reformatory at Redhill was asked, "What kind of work do the boys do in your reformatory?"

The answer was: "The boys are employed mostly in farm work. Our staple industry is farm work and we make all the boys go through it some time or other. They all begin with that. When a boy first comes in, no matter his antecedents, he is put to farm work. It is very marvellous to see the physical effect upon town boys especially." (Adapted from an article by Bernard Elliott in *The Local Historian,* vol. 13, no. 2 [1978].)

Perhaps children would not have gotten into as much trouble had they had more opportunities to go to school but prior to 1870 it was still a rarity to go to school. Fortunately there are records existing that give glimpses of conditions in the schools of the day. Elizabeth

Firth was a student at Crofton Hall Girls School (Yorkshire). Aged 15 in 1812, she kept a diary which has been preserved. Here are a few excerpts from it for that year:

Apr. 12. Several of the ladies were sent to bed for losing at spelling. . .
" 19. All the drawers trunks and pockets were searched for some cake that was taken out of Miss Hithe's drawer. . .
May 4. Miss Outhwaite was sent to bed at 7 for having her feet within the fender. . .
" 6. All the ladies who spoke after tea had a task. . .
" 8. We began of going to bed without candles. . .
" 12. My Governess told our class of Geography that if we did not know the rivers off we might go away. . .
" 14. We had dictionary excused and played on the grass. . .
" 18. Miss Bitton had her dirty clothes pinned to her back for having them under her bed. . .
" 19. Miss Wilson had the cap on for losing a French book. . .

Apparently food wasn't always the best, even in good schools. The Wesleyan Methodists founded Woodhouse Grove School (near Bradford), Yorkshire, in 1812. Here is what happened in 1823:

One day a boy was passing through the scullery, and saw the ladle used for the porridge in the swill tub. . .great indignation was aroused, and it was resolved. . .to refuse the porridge when next it was served out. Accordingly, on the next occasion, the 'pobs'. . .were refused by the bigger boys. . .and their example was followed by the middle boys; whilst the little ones of eight and nine years. . .looked wistfully at it, but only some half-dozen, fresh from a mother's tender care, found that their appetites were too strong. . .and with tears in their eyes gave way. At the mid-day meal all the little ones gave way, and at the third and closing meal of the day several of the middle-aged boys surrendered. Next morning several of the lads were sick, and at breakfast Mr Stamp. . .announced that no food would be given until the porridge, the same which had been three times previously placed before them, was eaten. . . at prayer. . . it was the practice for the boys to repeat the Lord's prayer audibly after the governor. But on this occasion not a sound was heard but the governor's voice, until he came to one of the petitions, when the whole school vociferated 'Give us this day our daily bread', and they left the governor to finish the prayer. . .

At dinner time on the second day a few others gave in. By this time the stuff on the plates was falling to pieces. . . Many of those who had surrendered. . . saved some portion of their bread for their brothers and friends. A gloom was settling on the school; even the biggest boys began to be ill. It might become a case of starvation to death. On the second night many boys were sleepless. The third morning came, when very few, and those the oldest and highest boys in the school, occupied the position of 'protestants' against the porridge. On this morning the stuff was found to be so offensive that the govenor wisely gave way, and permitted all the boys to have their regular food. [From C.W. Towlson, *Woodhouse Grove School, 1812-1962* (Leeds, 1962), pp. 23-24, quoting J.T. Slugg, *Woodhouse Grove School, Memorials and Reminiscences.* (Manchester, 1885)]

The compulsory education system which began in 1870 did not start of itself. It took a lot of agitation by a lot of courageous people over a considerable period of time to lead up to it.

One of these courageous souls was James Hole. Among his many reform movements he established a Ragged School to try to educate some of the very poor children living in Leeds, Yorkshire. The first one was established in 1859 at Richmond Hill, where certain children were given a brief education, food, and sometimes lodgings and were assisted in gaining employment. Below, Mr. Hole describes three of the children he brought into the school:

THE RAGGED SCHOOL CHILDREN

No. 1.-A.B., aged 12 years. . .His father died two months before A.B. was born. His mother lived a life of prostitution afterwards. She was very anxious that we should take her boy, and save him. . .A.B. was taken by his mother from beerhouse to beerhouse; they were often turned out of bad houses in the middle of the night. . .was taught by a man to pick the pockets of gentlemen of their handkerchiefs as they passed through the streets; has frequently said that had he not come here he would have been in prison long ago. . .When he came to us at first, was almost too weak to walk; was in rags. . .did not know anything of reading or writing. . .

No.3.-C.D. 12 years old, was born at C-, at which place his father, who was a farmer, died; mother came to Leeds five years since with three boys, - became a drunken prostitute; the boys had to beg and steal for their living, also gathered coals for their mother. I first met with them in. . .street; all of them were exceedingly ragged, C.D. had on an old tunic and trousers, with nothing more. He had the appearance of a child just dropping into the grave from want. His habits were filthy, destructive, idle, and vicious,-would gather potato parings in the street and eat them. When he first came to us he ran away three times. Mother was frequently out all night with men, leaving her children at the fireside,-they had no bed to lie down upon. They were often taken to the 'Casino'. I called upon the mother the Sunday before opening the school; the boys saw me, and ran in to tell their mother; she used horrible language to them, not knowing that I was at the door. . .

No.6.-G.H., 11 years old. Father died in the cholera, since which his mother lived the life of a prostitute, and of beastly drunken habits; for years has had no home for her children; has four boys. G.H. and I.J. have frequently been to prison. . .These four lads, with their mother, lodged in a cellar-dwelling. . .
[From J. Hole, *Light, More Light* (Woburn Reprint, 1969), 141-145]

The three foregoing examples of nineteenth-century school life are taken from *Yorkshire Schools and Schooldays,* University of Leeds Institue of Education, paper no. 14, January 1976.

A Dame School in the early 19th century

William Shaw, the proprietor of Bowes Academy, Yorkshire, paid damages of £300 to both a Mr. Jones and a Mr. Ockaby, whose sons had contracted ophthalmia while in his charge, and through negligence lost their sight.

The cross-examination revealed the appalling conditions at the school. Boys slept four and five at a time in flea-ridden beds covered by only one sheet and a quilt. More than 250 boarders had to wash themselves at a communal trough - soap was issued only on Saturdays - and had to dry themselves on the two towels provided each day. Many of them suffered from the itch.

The sanitary arrangements were equally primitive. There was a great tub in the middle of the room, and the tub was often full to overflowing. The food was disgusting. Such meat as came their way was often full of maggots; dry bread with watered milk was their tea, and then nothing was provided until an equally meagre breakfast.

APART FROM THE UNACCOUNTABLE concealment from the parents of the state of the boys' eyes, the judge did not seem at all concerned by the way they were taught, fed, housed and disciplined. His general view was that the conditions were consistent with the fees charged. "There was nothing to impeach the general conduct of Mr. Shaw in the management of the school."

When one considers that conditions were little better at the most expensive boarding schools, such as Elton and Harrow, and that flogging was the normal way of punishing not only boys but soldiers and sailors, perhaps it was not surprising that the judge accepted the conditions at Bowes Academy as being near enough to normal.

It was, after all, an age when brutality and ignorance were commonplace; with public hangings, cruel sports, child labour, and transportation for poaching. Even the Public Health Act of 1848 was not implemented until some 20 years later.

One imagines that for every case of this kind brought to Court, a dozen or more escaped attention. A large proportion of these children had no-one interested in their welfare. Why else should most of the advertisements have included the sinister phrase: "No vacations"? To put it bluntly, they were either illegitimate, or orphans. Once at a school they were completely at the mercy of the staff.

Privately - owned schools were not answerable to any governing body, nor did the staff have to be qualified. They existed for the same reason that baby farms existed - because there was a demand for their services.

BOWES ACADEMY HAD BEEN RUN by Mr. Shaw for 16 years before his conviction in 1823. His advertisements, and those of his competitors, remained virtually unchanged for many years. A typical example is reproduced in full:

EDUCATION, by Mr. SHAW; at Bowes Academy, near Greta-bridge, Yorkshire. Youth are carefully instructed in the English, Latin, and Greek Languages; writing, common and decimal arithmetic; book-keeping, mensuration, surveying, geometry, geography, and navigation; with the most useful branches of the mathematics; and are provided with board, clothes, and every necessary, at 20 guineas per annum each. No extra charges whatever. No vacations, except by the parents' desire. N.B. The French language 2 guineas per annum extra. Further particulars may be known on application to Mr. Timberlake, 25 Great Marylebonestreet: Mr. Annison, 10 Bedford-court, Covent-garden: and Mrs. Young, Ploughyard, Crown-street, Soho. Mr. Seaton, agent, 91, Whitecross-street, St. Luke's near Finsbury-square. All letters must be post paid. Mr. Shaw is in town, and attends daily at the George and Blue Boar, High Holborn, from 12 to 2 o'clock.

The syllabus is impressive, and pennypinching parents and guardians would have been reassured by the information that there were no extras. The clause about vacations was open to various interpretations. Those who did not wish to see their children again need not do so; others could make their own arrangements.

CHILDREN'S DRESS IN 1840

As we have seen, there were many changes that took place in this century. Over the centuries, however, some things have not changed. One of these is love. Following is a letter from one Winifred Waldron Goodeve to Moses Miall arranging for an elopement with him. Winifred seems to have been of a middleclass family. The places mentioned are in Hampshire, on the south coast.

May 5th, 1802.

My dear Miall,

Why did you not write to Foster on Monday? when I might have known his answer to-day-to-morrow it will be no doubt be all solved. Mr. and Mrs. White came up last evening; by Mr. W. I understand you cannot gain a license without a bondsman for your making a good husband! ha-ha, so my good sir you must bring a surety to the minister with you. A thought occurs to me that I think will obviate every difficulty, that an application to Mr. Bingham of Gosport for the license will be much better than to Mr. Clifton when we might be married at Alverstoke without hesitation as Bingham cannot refuse a license nor Clifton to marry us. If you can contrive to come over before twelve tomorrow morning I daresay to act such a part and perhaps it will be much better him than W. I shall not be over in the morng. probably. Do not forget the fetter that is to bind me to you or else if you offend I may chance to seek better quarters. I wish you well through your difficulties. My sister thinks I had better go away early in the morning from my own house and meet you at Stoke. Mr. W. is very much against our going to Stoke's Bay, the danger of going there he says is more than I imagine so that it may be much better for you to land beyond Blockhouse Point near to Haslar Hospital and walk to Stoke that way; what do you think of this plan? I hope to see you to-morrow and settle everything and will you enquire of

Ann if she has heard of any servant for Aunt Norton yet. Bring word down with you. I am as full of business as yourself. Adieu love.

Yours

W. W. Goodeve.

Marriage recordings have always been a temptation for parish clerks. This one is taken from the parish of Marown on the Isle of Man in 1823:

Married at Marown after a tedious courtship of nine days, Thos. Collister, The How, Rushen, a sporting widower of 60 to Mrs. Ann Lewin, a bouncing widow of 50 of Marown. 5 weeks have scarcely escaped since the bridegroom buried his former rib.

According to the following example, the bishop of the diocese of Salisbury, Wiltshire, ordered that the two children listed below be recorded as illegitimate even though the parents had gone through a marriage ceremony before hand:

Parish registers of Tisbury, Wilts:

5 Nov 1815 Samuel and Emilia, children of Eliza Gerrid of Tisbury
Bastards by order of the bishop
These children are the offspring of William Gerrid who married his own son's widow which is unlawful.

Besides the familiar parish registers, such as those quoted above, there is another source of information about your ancestors of the nineteenth century-censuses.

The nineteenth century had begun with the first accurate count of your English ancestors. This took place in 1801. Local officials such as schoolmasters, priests, and other educated persons visited each household and recorded the number of inhabitants. This has been done each ten years since then (except the war year of 1941) and regularly arouses suspicions among freedom-loving ancestors.

By 1841, it had been decided to record names, occupations and ages (to the lowest five-year term for persons aged over fifteen) and to tell whether each person had been born in that county or not. No doubt this aroused further suspicions in your ancestors' minds but it was only to provide valuable statistical information.

Ploughing in the early 19th Century.
(*From Pyne*, 1803.)

In 1851 even more information was required of your ancestor. This time he had to give precise ages, a relationship to the head of the house, and a precise place of birth. Since most people could still not read or write, the enumerator had to write down what he thought your ancestor said.

Every ten years your ancestor's suspicion was again aroused as the enumerator came around.

Agricultural Labourer at Work: early 19th Century.
(From Pyne, circa 1810.)

The numbers of Englishmen were greatly reduced from time to time by plagues and epidemics. Through the centuries, there were fairly regular outbreaks of cholera, and one of the worst occurred in 1832. Houses were small and cramped, sanitation was poor and drainage was very bad.

Many of your ancestors lived in cellars where sewage seeped through the walls. One small village in Northumberland, called Newburn, lost 10 per cent of its population that year.

The twin towns of Gateshead and Newcastle, straddling the Durham-Northumberland border, had 497 deaths from cholera in 1832 and a total of 801 deaths before the epidemic finally subsided:

In the same yard the steps leading down to the river itself were covered at high water and here river filth found a resting place. Drainage from the church land and that above it soaked down under the houses and through the narrow passages; there was no privy accommodation; many of the passages and rooms were badly lit. The passages also contained open gutters which eventually connected with those in Hill Gate; a "filth corner" where rubbish was deposited for collection by the public scavengers, undoubtedly aided the blocking of the open gutters . . . .

An event that took place in the late 1830's illustrates the conditions that prevailed at the time of the epidemic. This was the building of Victoria Street. "Victoria Street was formerly the site of a stone quarry, filled with rubbish and refuse, which was allowed to be 'shot' at so much per load when the quarry was worked out. When the cavity was more than filled the street was built. It was never paved and one house later housed thirty people of five families. Two underground rooms, partially lighted by sunken windows, housed two families 'like pigs in a sty.' The liquid contents from the privy and ashpit oozed through the walls of one room". [T.W. Ede, "Cholera in Gateshead and Newcastle. 1831-1832," *Durham County Local History Society,* Bulletin 14 (March 1972): 31]

Cholera, brought in from Europe and Asia, naturally hit the seaport towns first before spreading inland. The plague produced its heroes, as do all such crises and some of them are your ancestors. Their names never cross anyone's lips, but they are equally as heroic as the Florence Nightingales and the Captain Oates' of their day. One of these individuals was a Reverend John Aubone Cook, who was first a curate at St. Margaret's Westminster. In the cholera epidemic of 1848/49 he visited the sick regularly, and in one week in 1849 buried fifty of his parishioners. The next year he was transferred to the parish of South Benfleet in Essex, where within two years he had the same problem he had had in Westminster. Again he worked endlessly. One story taken from an article by H.E. Priestley in *Essex Countryside,* should illustrate his qualities:

> A traveller who had been taken ill with the cholera had fallen by the wayside and lay helpless. Nobody dared touch him or go near him for fear of catching it, but the news of the poor man's plight spread by word of mouth through the village. In the end one of the parishioners, a nonconformist, boldly approached him and helped him to his feet. As the two passed slowly along the village street not a single householder would open his door to them.
>
> 'Try the vicarage,' shouted one from the distance. 'That's the only place where he'll be taken in.'
>
> Slowly the two men mounted the hill to the vicarage. When they reached the door the poor traveller collapsed, shrieking in agony. The vicar came to the door and the two, vicar and nonconformist, carried him upstairs and put him to bed, where he was nursed until he recovered.

Even after the cholera epidemic had subsided he had many other problems in that low-lying marshland. He died a few years later at the ripe old age of forty-seven, completely exhausted, I suppose.

Some people are known to have written their own epitaphs before they died. Joseph Dawson, a blacksmith, died 16 September 1818, aged 74, at Louth (Lincolnshire). It is not known if he wrote his own epitaph or not, but it is still colorful:

> My sledge and hammer lie declin'd,
> My bellows too have lost their wind,
> My fire's extinct, my forge decayed,
> My vice is in the dust all laid.
> My coal is spent, my iron gone,
> My nails are drove, my work is done.
> My fire dry'd corpse lies here at rest,
> My soul smoke-like soars to be blest.
> [From *The Epitaphs in St. Mary's Churchyard, Louth*]

There are other versions of these lines, adapted slightly to the person's occupation.

While some of your ancestors may have died in epidemics, others may have given their lives in defense of their country. England was threatened several times in the nineteenth century.

Many Britishers still remember the threat of German invasion after the fall of France in World War II. A similar situation existed in 1802/03 when local militia groups were frantically increased and trained to repel an expected Napoleonic invasion.

Very similar to the VE and VJ victory days of World War II came the celebration of victory over Napoleon in 1814 and of Waterloo in 1815. The towns and parishes celebrated with feasts on the commons or the parish green, where the poor were treated to the popular roast beef, plum pudding, and beer. These feasts were followed by a burning in effigy of Napoleon, a man who had troubled Europe for twenty years.

Many of your ancestors saw naval action. Large numbers of men were serving at the time of the Battle of Trafalgar.

All English schoolboys are familar with Nelson's message before the battle. Few know the circumstances as to how the exact wording originated:

Lord Nelson, 1758-1805. Admiral, notable for his victories at the Nile, 1798: Copenhagen, 1801, and Trafalgar, 1805.

H.M.S. Victory, Lord Nelson's Flagship at Trafalgar, A typical "Wooden Wall" of old England.

Death of Nelson at the Battle of Trafalgar, 1805

21 OCTOBER, 1805

NELSON went on deck, and mounting the poop ordered certain signals to be made, and at about a quarter to twelve he said, "Mr. Pasco, I wish to say to the Fleet, "ENGLAND CONFIDES THAT EVERY MAN WILL DO HIS DUTY," and he added, "You must be quick, for I have one more to make, which is for "Close Action." Pasco replied, "If your Lordship will permit me to substitute EXPECTS for CONFIDES the signal will soon be completed because the word EXPECTS is in the vocabulary but CONFIDES must be spelled". Nelson replied in hast, and with seeming satisfaciton, "That will do, Pasco, make it directly".
THE LIFE OF NELSON, (Sir Geoffrey Callender)

Were your ancestors coal miners? If so, they led a precarious working life underground and lived in very mean hovels on the surface. They were very brave men, each day's work being a battle against the forces of nature. The word **winning** when referring to coal mining is well chosen. Many lost their lives not only through accidents, but through eye and lung diseases.

The Lundhill Yorkshire Colliery explosion is an example of the dangerous conditions under which they lived and worked. At the time of the disaster, which occurred on 19 February 1857, there were 200 men and boys underground, 189 of whom were killed. Ninety women lost their husbands in the tragedy, and 220 children were left fatherless. At that time, the miners who worked at the mine, or pit, used both safety lamps and candles, and they were permitted to decide personally when it was safe to use one or the other. It was stated after the catastrophe that although the current of air entering the mine was adequate, there was no ventilating current at the coal face. Moreover, standards of management underground were unsatisfactory, the method of working the coal was dangerous, and the colliery's general and special rules were blatantly disregarded.

The disaster at the Oaks Colliery, near Barnsley, Yorkshire on the twelfth and thirteenth of December 1866 was Yorkshire's worst mine disaster, and one of the most terrible catastrophes in British mining history. The disaster took the lives of 361 men and boys. Of the 340 persons in the mine at the time of the first explosion on Wednesday, 12 December, only six ultimately survived. Twenty seven rescue workers were killed by a second explosion of gas on the following morning.

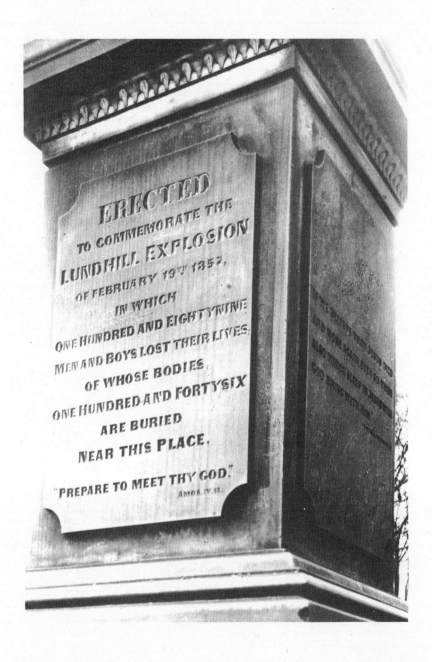

Asked about the colliery when he was giving evidence before the Royal Commission of 1881, John Edward Mammatt, hero of the Oaks, remarked that some eighty bodies were still unaccounted for:

7425   *Are the men quite reconciled to it?--Oh, yes, we never hear anything of it now.*

7426   *All all these are entombed in the pit?--We have a different set of men at the colliery now.*

7427   *Have you been there very often, and have you found whether there was much difficulty in overcoming that sentimental feeling?--For a few months there was that feeling, but it has quite died out. We sometimes come across some bones, we did the other day, and we sent them up to the top, but nobody claimed them, and they were buried; there was only a skull and a piece of leg bone.*

Sentiment, then, had taken second place to bread and butter, as it must. There would have been no benefit to the Barnsley area if the mine had been permanetly closed. There could be no fitting monument, certainly not that of an abandoned colliery, to the men and boys of the Oaks.

(**Left to right, back row:** Hy. Wraithmell, Friend Senior, Willie Lightowler; **front row:** Squire Shires, John Garfitt, Richard Wood, J. Mallinson.)

The above photograph shows seven survivors of the disaster which occurred at Combs Pit, Thornhill, near Dewsbury, Yorkshire, on 4 July 1893. These men were rescued after being entombed for thirty hours, but their 139 workmates who had descended with them were all killed. The disaster was caused by the ignition of methane gas by a naked flame. The county's pits were sometimes known as "gasometers," for they were amongst the most fiery in the country. [See *Studies in the Yorkshire Coal Industry,* by Robert G. Neville Hendon Publishing Co., Nelson, Lancs., 1976)

Coal miners are probably the most misunderstood of all occupational groups. When one considers the long fights they had for decent wages and less dangerous working conditions, the humbleness of their homes, the poor food they had to nourish them while performing hard manual labor and the constant risk they faced of injury and death, he must rank them, in bravery and hardships encountered, with the men who sailed on masted ships.

Some seams were only 33 inches high. The miners had to work in a prone position. The seams were not always dry, and the water dripping from the roof or coming up through the floor was very impure and caused boils and other skin diseases. Small wonder then that sometimes the miner lived it up on weekends at the local pub. But so did the sailor home from the sea.

Many of your mining ancestors were men of more than average intelligence, talented in a variety of fields. The colliery brass bands are evidence of this. The idea that all colliers needed was a pick and shovel and muscle to use it is far from true. A slight mistake in judgement of roof conditions could cause a high loss of life and production. Mining ancestors developed a sixth sense, a sense for safety. This sixth sense had to be developed in one's youth, and it grew as his experience with more dangerous work grew. For this reason the Coal Mines Act did not allow anyone to *start* work in the coal mines if he were older than eighteen years.

Although the accompanying photograph is dated 12 September 1935 and thus does not really belong to the nineteenth century, it illustrates that the coal miner was as warm a family man as anyone else. The photograph was taken after an explosion at the North Gawber Colliery, Yorkshire in which nineteen men were killed. Apparently, one miner had time to write a message to his wife - "Farewell Fanny old pet" - before being overtaken. (See Robert G. Neville, *Yorkshire Miners in Camera.*)

In the 1978 winter issue of the *Journal of the Bristol and Avon Family History Society,* Patricia Lindegaard writes an article about the coal miners in south Gloucestershire in 1841.

An Elijam Waring makes a report on the employment of young persons in the mines and records the following:

> 'The extreme narrowness of the seams, in some cases, as at Yate Common, where the coal is only one foot thick, altogether precludes adults from cutting it out, and the work is therefore performed by young lads whose size is more suited to the contracted space. The mode of drawing the tubs into the mainway (is) by a girdle of rope round the loins, attached to the load by a hook and chain. (This) struck me so painfully at first that I was induced to examine closely into its effects on the frame conceiving it to be a barbarous and unnatural manner of applying muscular power.'

This examination was pronounced satisfactory however, and Waring stated that the colliers themselves preferred the girdle and chain to the shoulder strap tug. One of them said

> 'Every country do like his own way best.'

Some pits were praised and other criticised. Easton had a commodious hutch where seven men and two or three boys could go up and down, snugly protectd from jets of water, as well as from stones falling on them. But, at the miserably wet pit at Cromhall,

> 'I saw the poor fellows coming up in the Coal Tubs at mid-day to escape suffocation from bad air in the stalls, smeared with clay and dripping with shaft water from which they protected themselves partially by hanging old sacks on their heads and shoulders.'

Current wages of the adult colliers were from 18s to 20s per week when in full work. Lads from 14 to 18 earned from 7s to 12s and boys under 13 from 2s to 6s per week, according to age and capabilities.

> 'Many of the boys appear to be wretchedly paid for their labour by the low renumeration of 3d or 4d a day.'

Hours of work varied from eight to ten hours daily, though the night shift was from 6 pm to 6 am the following morning. On the credit side,

> 'There appears to be an "esprit de corps" among the colliers which attaches their progeny to the work as a sort of hereditary calling, distinguished by a degree of adventure, from its exposure to danger and the abandonment of daylight.'

However, an eight year old orphan, about to be sent down the pit for the first time, was asked by Waring how he liked the thoughts of it.

> 'Not at "aal", sir', replied the boy.

Waring comments,

> 'What could such a poor little desolate fellow do, but submit to his allotment with whatever sinkings of heart at its gloomy and unnatural character?'

He adds, 'I have often thought of him with compassion.'

The latter part of the report contains examinations of the managers of the Coal Pits and the workers themselves.

> John Harvey: is a carter in Crown Pit. (Mr. Water's); says he is 13; looks not more than 9 or 10. The men say they know him to be the age he states; draws coal with another boy about 2 hundredweights at a time; eight score yards on rails with slides underneath the cart; does not catch cold or lose his appetite; earns 6d a day or thereaway; gets

potatoes and butter or potatoes fried with bacon when he gets home from the pit; gets whatever he can catch; is always very hungry after work; seldom has as much as he could eat; does not go to Sunday School because he has no clothes besides what he works in; cannot read; never had a pair of shoes or stockings in his life.

Mr. Waters, the employer, said that he had heard of this boy once going without food for two or three days, a situation he would not have allowed had he known of it in time. Waring said that Harvey had a drunken father and an improvident mother, *'What a deplorable lot!'*, he said. By contrast:

George Chambers, *aged 11. Works in the same pit with Harvey; is taller by the head, though two years younger: is Harvey's partner in carting. Has a mother who takes good care of him. Goes to the Sunday School and to Church at Siston. This boy has a healthy appearance.*

Abraham Carter, *10 years old. "Do push with another boy". Has worked twelve months in the pit; earns only 3d a day. Can read a little; does not go to Sunday School; has no shoes; complains of tightness in the chest; looks delicate.*

Samuel Britton, *carter, aged 18. Has worked 11 years; now earns 9s a week. Can stand upright in most parts of the pit. Cannot read and does not go to Sunday School. This is a robust well grown lad with a healthy countenance.*

John Palmer, *aged about 15, Carter. Earns 5s a week. Works always at night; has done so for the past two years. Gets his sleep in the day-time. Goes to the pit at six in the evening and remains there until six next morning. Can read the Bible and goes to the Moravian Sunday School at Kingswood Hill. This lad looks pale, but otherwise has no indications of unhealthiness such unnatural hours of work considered.*

George Woodington, *aged 7½. Has been working one year as a door boy. This infantine labourer has never been taught his letters but attends a place of worship with his father. I went to the mouth of Easton Pit and saw the urchin emerge from the hutch with his father, his white cheeks strongly contrasting with the coal dust smeared over them; he had his candlestick in front of his cap like all the rest. The poor little fellow answered my questions cheerfully and seemed quite naturalised in his doleful vocation. There was something at once grotesque and revolting in the workmanlike demeanour of this pygmy collier. His father assured me he had been with him in the pit for twelve months.*

Daniel Poole, *aged 50. Has been a collier all his life; earns 13s a week cutting coal in Soundwell Pit. Is learning to read in the Moravian Sunday School. Has nine children and would send them all to school on Sundays if they had decent clothes. Finds it hard to maintain so many, provisions being so dear. Likes to keep himself and his family clean and wholesome. Thinks colliers are better men nowadays than they used to be.*

The following poem may refer to an early twentieth-century family but it applies equally to the late nineteenth century. It describes a coal-mining family. It originally appeared in *The Dalesman,* a Yorkshire periodical.

Home Were Never t'Same

I grew up as a miner's son,
I mind them days were 'ard,
But us the kids we 'ad us fun,
Like scrappin' int' backyard.

Me mam an 'dad 'ud rise at four
An' she'd go off t'mill,
An' then me dad 'ud slam the door
An' set off up the 'ill.

Us kids 'ud snuggle under t'clothes
An' snooze till t'mornin' light,
Then Sal 'ud scream: "It's six tha' knows
Art' sleepin' till tonight?"

We'd all shout "Aye!" and then we'd laugh,
Till Tom stripp'd t'bed o' t' sheets,
I'd thump 'is ear, and' call 'im daft,
An' say "wait till toneet."

We'd run down t'stairs, pull on us boots
I'd grab me book an' rule,
While Tom set off t'factory tools,
Sal saw us kids to school.

At four o'clock we'd all dash back,
Last 'ome 'ud be a nit,
I'd skip thro' t'yard, kick 'tatie sack,
An' shout: "our Jim's a twit!"

Me mam 'ud stand outside back gate,
An' kiss us as we came,
Then tell us off for bein' late,
An' kiss us all again!

As night drew on, front gate 'ud bang,
Me mam 'ud get stove lit,
Big hob-nail boots down t'passage rang,
It were me dad from t'pit.

Ee'd bustle in wi' mucky face,
An' slump down on't settee,
We'd all shift round from t'fireplace,
Ee'd tek Sam on 'is knee.

"Now wheer's me tea, an' wheer's
      thi mam?"
Were allus first he said,
"Me mam's in t'back boilin' that lamb
We gor on t'tick wi t'bread."

I'd spend me night not doin' owt,
Me dad ud go t'pub,
Me mam 'ud sew up 'is pit coat,
An' Tom 'ud go t' club.

An' then came t'war; I got called up,
Our Sal were wed that year,
I 'ere our Sam 'ad 'is first sup,
Me dad took bad wi t'beer.

I got no leave, two years from France,
But then me papers came,
I dived down't street an' damn near
      danced,
But 'ome were never t'same...
[Pauline Mary Scanlan]

Early Nineteenth-century Carbon Range

Bulletin 14 (March 1972) of the *Durham County Local History Society* carries a good description of a coal-mining village as it would have appeared in the late 1800s and early 1900s.

By 1905 every house in the District had some sort of sanitary convenience though many required improvement. The inferior, monotonously-uniform houses faced onto unmade streets with little or no space at the back except for that allotted to privy or earth closet and coal house. Kitchen and human waste were collected by cart, at first by farmers who only came when no other tasks required their attention and later by more regular "midden men." Obnoxious smells were cloaked by ashes. Ashes, post stone, or coal duff were used to fill ruts and pot holes. Flies, mice and rats abounded-it was not yet universally recognised that they brought disease and death. Each summer had its epidemic of scarlet fever, diphtheria or occasionally typhoid. The wooden-slatted pantry ventilators opened on to back streets where in the germ-laden air, bread and "stotty cakes" cooled on window sills or door steps.

The houses themselves could be spotless with ochre or red stepstone liberally applied to the entrance. The blackleaded range, the gleaming brass of rails and candlesticks, and the shining steel of the heavy fender and fire irons all bore testimony to the slavish devotion of the women folk. The water supply--or lack of it--was a factor of prime importance. Private wells and water carts supplied this need at first, and for many years before each house had its own piped supply, the communal stand pipe--as few in number as two to a village--served an essential purpose. Water was carried in pails and the water pail always stood on the pantry shelf in readiness for domestic use. In the absence of children for water carrying, the lifting and carting of heavy pails was women's work. The rain butt, fed from the gutters, collected a welcome supply of soft water in this "hard" area and was used for woollens and hairwashing.

Essential furniture included the square deal table, centrally placed in the room with a wooden form standing behind it for the use of the children, two or three wooden chairs with a "cracket" or stool, and a rocking chair. A large press, set of drawers or desk bed completed the heavy furniture of this room. The heavy mantel shelf, with its brass or tasselled border hiding an extra airing rail, would be decorated with photographs, candlesticks, china dogs, pottery souvenirs or other knick-knackery. The floor, scrubbed clean, was covered with home made mats - "clippy" or "hooky" according to the preference of the housewife or the ability of her helpers. The wooden mat frames would perhaps stand in the corner, or if there was "a mat in" the assembled construction would be poised across two chair backs with a supply of clippings and a number of woodenhandled, shining steel proggers ready for anyone who wished to give assistance. Reward for this endeavour was a supply of home-made toffee already broken up in its tray.

The home was very much the women's world and work was not often undertaken by women outside the home. Families were large and took some looking after. The men of the house came home black with coal-dust, tired and ravenously hungry. While they washed in front of the fire, their pit clothes would be "dadded" against the wall outside in readiness for the next day. Cooking without modern aids was almost a continous process as menfolk came for their main meal at different times and traditionally did not lift a finger to help until fed and washed. To its eternal shame, Murton Colliery takes credit for the introduction of the night shift to this coal field, to recoup some of the £ 1/2m. lost during its sinking.

The men folk spent most of their off duty time talking about, thinking about, and dreaming about the pit. This was very natural as the chances were very high that every male companion was similarly employed. The knocker-up was the first of the fraternity to rise each morning. The other village dignitary was the crakeman who wandered the rows later in the day announcing colliery news or union meetings. There was not a lot of spare time and each man spent his according to his tastes--it might be over drinks at the club or pub or playing fives, football, quoits or billiards; the less energetic hobby of pigeon keeping attracted groups of men around the landing area in front of the "crees," some leaning against the wooden supports but more, by habit, on their "hunkers," a pose adopted of necessity when resting from their daily work. If men "were chapel" then bible class, playing in the brass band, or membership of the ambulance team would be more likely to appeal as a pastime. Otherwise gambling at pitch and toss, racing whippets or greyhounds, or poaching with tamed ferrets were the only possible activities.

Children did not remain young and irresponsible for long. Unlike their modern counterparts, the least sophisticated activities seemed to keep them absorbed for long periods. They played games, romped the woods and scrambled over the tips: boys bowled girths and made "titchy burners," girls played at houses and at infinite varieties of hopscotch: holidays away from home were unknown and the larger part of a child's programme would be filled by helping father and mother or working for someone else who might be prepared to give them coppers in exchange. . . . The short childhood terminated abruptly with the labour exam where a minimum literacy test was a premature passport to an adult world of toil. This was a school leaving certificate of a special kind. The cleverer the child the sooner he could dispense with his education. [W.E. Moyes, "Easington Rural District," pp. 8-11]

Was your ancestor a footman, a butler, or a maidservant in a middle-or upper-class household? There were almost one and a half million such persons in the late 1800s. This number increased in the early 1900s before economic conditions changed.

Domestic service thrived for two main reasons. First, because economic necessity forced larger poor families to put their children--meaning, mostly, their daughters--into service as one of the few means of feeding and clothing them, and putting a roof over their heads. Second, because servants "knew their place" and accepted it as their lot in life to serve their betters.

Parlourmaid in afternoon black dress with crinoline; starched white apron and fancy cap. *c.* 1860.

In 1891, according to the Official Census, the servant class was among the largest groups of the working population: 1,386,167 females and 58,527 males were indoor servants in private homes and out of a population of twenty-nine million in England and Wales. Of these, 107, 167 girls and 6,891 boys in service were aged between **ten** and fifteen years. These children were put to work from dawn until late at night for a few shillings a month and perhaps one-half day off a week if they had considerate employers. They were required to wear uniform or livery, and their lives were regulated by strict rules. They slept in barely-furnished attics and lived and worked in the dark lower regions of the big Victorian houses and stately homes. They had separate entrances (below ground), separate staircases (at the back of the house) and lives separate from those of their employers.

They were treated abominably by our present standards, not necessarily because they were cruelly treated but because for the most part they were regarded as inferior beings. Servants were used to seeing people laughing and talking and being agreeable to one another all around them, while at the same time ignoring them entirely. . . .

Cook, Footman, Housemaid and Page. Page in typical short, tight tunic with rows of buttons. 1847.

Whole armies of butlers, cooks and housemaids were employed in the great households of Victorian and Edwardian England, plus the battalions of grooms, coachmen and gardeners employed outdoors. At the turn of the twentieth century, the kitchen staff at the Duke of Portland's home at Welbeck Abbey comprised a steward, wine butler, under butler, groom of chambers, four royal footmen, two steward's room footmen, master of the servants' hall, two pageboys, head chef, second chef, head baker, second baker, head kitchen maid, two under kitchen maids, sundry vegetable maids and scullery maids, head stillroom maid, hall porter, two hallboys, kitchen porters and six odd-job men. The Duke also employed a head housekeeper, a valet, a personal maid for the Duchess, his daughter's personal maid, head nursery governess, tutor, French governess, schoolroom footman and fourteen housemaids. There were six engineers and four firemen to look after the steam heating and the new-fangled electric plant, a telephone clerk and assistant, a telegrapher and three night watchmen.

Outdoors there were more than thirty servants in the stables and a similar number employed in the newly installed garage, although it was more than a decade ahead of the time when the motor car would oust the horse-drawn carriage. Other servants worked in the gardens, home farm, gymnasium, golf course and laundry. Also, there was a head window cleaner and two assistant window cleaners. . . .

Servants in the great houses formed the aristocracy of domestic service. Most of those employed in the stately homes enjoyed comfortable standards of living and basked in the reflected glory of their high-born employers. But at the other end of the scale, no respectable villa in the suburbs was without its maid or maids, and the majority of those "in service" in Britain were employed by the middle classes, not the aristocracy. These servants were mostly children, the maids of the kitchens, the tweeny or between-maid and the boot-boys. They were mere chattels and slaves, whom their employers hardly ever saw, and frequently failed to recognize when they did.

True, a servant was paid a wage, although in the case of the lowest paid, a month's wages for a scullery maid in 1900 amounted to little more than ten shillings (50p), the cost of a good dinner at the best hotel in Brighton.

Also, unlike a slave, a servant was free to give notice and leave. But in practice, she or he was entirely dependent on the master for a "character," and without a satisfactory written reference from the previous employer a domestic servant stood no chance of finding another job. . .

The Testaments were used to convince the servants that it was God's will that they should stay in their places at the bottom of society, and asknowledge the superiority of those they served. Texts and tracts were showered on the servants' hall and the words of John Keble were enlisted to the cause of subordination:

> The trivial round, the common task,
> Will furnish all we need to ask,
> Room to deny ourselves, a road
> To bring us daily nearer God. . . .

But "love thy neighbour" did not mean treat him as an equal. The have-nots were after all part of the Divine order of things, to be saved from themselves with the Word and bowls of nourishing soup, but kept at arm's length. The barriers were maintained even in church. The middle classes, following the Royal example, took their servants to Sunday service with them, and nobody saw anything in the least questionable about the fact that the domestics were made to sit apart from their employers in separate pews, usually at the back of the church. . . .

. . .Mrs. Dorothy Shaw, of Newbury, who started as a tweeny in the previous year, says in a letter to the author that she once asked her mistress for a candle to light her attic bedroom. The lady cut a candle in half and gave one half to her with the remark: "I don't encourage my maids to read in bed." The usual ration was one candle a week for each servant. . . .

Yet even they were not as badly off as children who went into service half a century earlier. Elizabeth Simpson, born March, 1853, was one of them. At the age of ten she was sent as a kitchen maid to a large house near Harrogate in Yorkshire. She had to get up at 4 a.m. to scrub the stone floors of the dairy with cold water and turn the butter churns until her little arms ached. For most of the year she rose in the dark and worked by the light of a single candle which she pushed ahead of her as she moved across the stone flags on her knees.

She was kept hard at work throughout the day, blackleading grates, lighting fires, polishing floors with the slops from the chambermaid's pail to make them shine, waiting upon other servants, until at 9 p.m. she crawled back to bed, again, for most of the year, by candlelight. It was a rule, strictly enforced, that she must never be seen by any of the family. If, by some mischance, they happened to meet, she must not speak to them, but curtsey and disappear as quickly as possible.

Few, if any, of these children could read or write, so we have no way of knowing how they felt. We can only guess at the effect on a child of ten of being taken away from her family and put into this harsh environment. . . .

. . .When she arrived at the big house where she was to work, she was so overawed by it all that she curtsied to the powdered footman who opened the door, thinking he was the gentleman of the house. She became the eighth of eight housemaids and slaved from 5 a.m. until late at night at all the roughtest work. She had to scrub at the bare boarded floors of the staff rooms with a mixture of soft soap and silver sand until her hands, and arms up to her elbows, were red raw. On most nights she cried herself to sleep.

Nanny in cap and apron with frilled straps. 1899.

To understand how children could be pressed into such servitude, one has to recall the general economic conditions of the time. In the 1890s thousands of Londoners were homeless, sleeping in the parks, on the Embankment or in the recesses of London Bridge. However badly a servant might be accommodated, it was no doubt better than the prevailing housing conditions for the poor in the London of the 1890s as described by a minister, Joseph Ritson, in the *Primitive Methodist Magazine.* Of seven hundred families in Marylebone, three-quarters were forced to live packed together like sardines in single rooms. In London as a whole there were 50,000 families, each occupying only a single room "and in most of them the conditions of health and morality are utterly absent." [Frank Dawes, *Not in Front of the Servants: A True Portrait of English Upstairs/Downstairs Life* (New York: Taplinger Publishing Co., 1974), pp. 9-17]

From this same book, we read:

No, of all servants the one most to be pitied was the single-handed maid in a lower middle class household, who hadn't even the consolation of seeing the grand life at second-hand. She lived a life of unremitting drudgery, made worse by almost total isolation from her own kind. It is not difficult to imagine the loneliness of a young girl of thirteen or fourteen, taken from the unceasing clamour and chatter of a large family and placed in a situation where she was alone for most of the time. These "cook-generals," the general dogsbodies of the suburbs, were expected to live in the kitchen as if it were really a servants' hall.

There was no outlet for the youthful high spirits of girls like this. One of the author's correspondents has written with great sympathy and insight of a maid-of-all-work employed at the turn of the twentieth century in her parents' home when there were seven young children to be looked after: "She was fifteen when she arrived and already had her hair 'pinned up,' which in that era meant she was grown up. She was a big, strong girl and she needed to be, as a good deal of hard work was expected of her. . . .On the few evenings when this poor girl had no work to do she would sit in a dimly-lit kitchen and knit horrible cotton lace with which she trimmed her calico underwear. Sometimes she would write a letter home and come into the living room to ask my mother if she might 'slip down to the box.' Fancy having to ask permission to post a letter. This 'slipping down to the box' often took some time, I imagine this lonely creature met and talked to boys. How she must have longed for people of her own to talk to! Once a month she went home for the day. She only lived about four miles away and I think she was able to get a horse bus part of the way. . ." [pp. 74-75]

The reports of various commissions appointed by Parliament provide a good summary of life in this eventful century:

Topics on which nineteenth century commissioners reported were many and varied: agriculture, transport (roads, trains, canals), charities, women and children, schools and churches, friendly societies and trades unions, landownership, the poor, public houses and theatres, to mention a few. Royal commissioners, appointed to report on a particular topic, visited a locality, took evidence, interviewing individuals and ascertaining local circumstances which had a bearing on their purpose. Over the span of a century, volumes ran into their hundreds, but among those I have found hitherto most rewarding, as regards the amount of local history therein contained, have been the following reports on:

1 the Education of the Poor (1818/1819)

2 Charities (1819-1840--Gloucestershire: 1828)

3   Poor Law (1834, 1862, 1873, 1909)

4   Roads (1840-1972)

5   Children's Employment (1842-1843, and Women: 1843, 1867-1869)

6   Friendly Societies (from 1852, but especially 1880)

7   Trades Unions (1867-1869)

8   Agriculture (1882, 1894)

9   Housing of the Working Classes (1885)

10   Canals (1906-1911)

A list of all owners of land in England and Wales (1872-1873) is also to be found, by county, in the 1874 series.

To give an example: whilst delving into these [parliamentary] papers to find out more about the village of Almondsbury near Bristol, where the family into which I was researching lived in the last century, I discovered a number of facts that I had not known previously. My image of village life there was considerably enlarged as a result: there had been an endowed school in the village, besides the dame's school and prior to the establishment of a National School in 1833, attended by about 20 children (only a small proportion of what must have been the total number, most of whom would have been at work on the land from a very tender age!); there was a provision in the early part of the century for the custom of distributing free bread to poor households at Christmas and Good Friday; even as late as the 1860's most village boys were working full-time on a farm by the time they were ten years of age; at the same time there was a night school run by the local schoolmaster five nights a week to teach the adult men how to read and write for there were a good number who could not; women could earn 10d to 1/- a day working in the fields, but a good number of them were employed in washing and charring [cleaning]; a period of dry weather was welcomed by the men, because when it was wet they were apt not be employed, nor paid, therefore; water supply and drainage were defective.

One report made towards the end of the 1860's highlights individuals, all interviewed by an assistant commissioner:

8. SOCIALISM IN HYDE PARK IN THE NINETIES.

A London Sweep with his "Climbing Boy," about 1845.

1) Albert Merritt . . . aged 10 the 21st June.

Has been working for farmer Carter; earned 3s. a week; drove plough; liked school better . . . would leave home at 5 or 5.30 a.m. . . . at work till noon; then got a quarter of an hour for dinner, bread and cheese and cider . . . did not get home till 7 o'clock; had his supper, potatoes and bacon, with nothing to drink. Goes to bed at 8 o'clock.'

2) Farmer Carter was at a meeting together with farmers Gayner, Thomas, Young and Gunter, presided over by the commissioner. These employers thought that to raise the working age to 13

'would inflict serious hardship on the parents, would embarass the farmer in the cultivation of the land, and would even be likely to lessen the future efficiency of the child as a labourer.'

3) The Reverend Thomas Murray-Browne was naturally far more concerned about the spiritual welfare of his flock:

'Milking in the yards where there is a herd of cattle is found in my long experience injurious to morals. I with this were restricted to men and boys; better still to men only.'

4) Likewise, Mr. William Powell, the schoolmaster, was anxious to exercise his profession efficiently:

'The large gaps in attendance are because of the demand for labour. Boys are frequently absent for 3 months in spring, bird-scaring and potato-planting, and again for 3 months in autumn, gleaning, potato and apple-picking. I should like to keep them regular till 11 years of age.'

Boys at work in a Coal-mine: one boy is pushing a truck of coal down a low passage way, whilst the other closes the door when the truck has passed.
(From Report of the Commission of 1842.)

5) John William, the parish clerk, claimed to be well acquainted with the feelings of the people:

'The average wage is about 12s. a week . . . A man's worst time is when he has five or six children . . . many families get fresh meat once a week on Sundays, but many a labourer might go through a week without even a bit of bacon. The staple food is bread and cheese. Most distress is caused by either a husband being given to drink, or a wife being a bad manager . . . Most farmers have a young man or two living in the house, hired by the year or half-year, generally at the "mop".' [Roy S. Walker, "Parliamentary Papers-An Untapped Source?" *Journal of the Bristol & Avon Family History Society,* no. 7 (Spring 1977): 15-16]

Inside a Cotton Factory. 1835.
(From Baines' "History of Cotton Manufacture.")

Chapter 5

USING CONTEMPORARY RECORDS IN COMPILING THE HISTORY OF RECENT GENERATIONS OF YOUR FAMILY

THE ENGLAND I REMEMBER

The England I remember
Had a slow and sturdy tread;
The blacksmith by his anvil,
The baker with his bread.
The horse-drawn plough proceeding
Along the hedge-ringed fields,
With sea-gulls calling loudly
For what the furrow yields.
The flower show and the market,
With lowing of the kine;
The graceful garden party,
We prayed the day be fine.
There was time for leisure
And dancing on the green,
For simple country pleasure
That could be heard and seen.
The village shops have vanished
And chain stores now abound,
The humble inn is banished
And can no more be found;
Tall buildings rise and darken
The lovely evening sky,
And we no longer hearken
To the barn owl's hooting cry,
O England I remember,
With your slow and sturdy tread,
The blacksmith's lucky horse-shoe
And the baker's crusty bread.

A. DE S. GEORGANO

This England (Summer 1977)

Now that you have warmed up to the fact that your ancestors are real people, you are ready to gather the material for writing their history. The logical place to start is in your home and in the homes of relatives. Gathering information from relatives based on their personal knowledge may be easy and is certainly economical. It should definitely be considered before you search original records.

Unfortunately, some people have carried out extensive and expensive research only to find out later that the same information was already in the hands of family members.

The importance of noting family traditions and of writing down facts you remember about your family, facts stated by relatives, and documentary evidence in the homes of relatives cannot be emphasized too strongly.

A most valuable approach to obtaining information from living relatives is through your own family organization. Such an organization should allow all its members easier access to documents and momentos which can provide valuable information for a written history.

Personal Knowledge

A tremendous amount of valuable knowledge is committed to memory and never written down. It is partially lost when the person's memory fails or becomes dim and is, of course, completely lost when the person dies. For this reason you should start immediately to contact living relatives to find out how much they know about their ancestry. Procrastination may make such information unobtainable later, although you may be able to obtain some of it elsewhere at high cost.

As you begin to contact living relatives, always consider visiting or writing the more elderly first. The older a person becomes, the more likelihood there is of his memory losing its sharpness, and yet a more elderly person is likely to have more valuable recollections concerning the family than a younger person might have.

Before visiting, prepare a list of the required items you wish to draw out so that no important point will be overlooked. Remember that just as individuals vary, so do memories. What may be clear in the memory of one individual may be far from clear in the memory of another. Give your relative ample opportunity to remember certain events and dates, and allow him to talk freely-even to wander off the subject now and then. Not too many people can readily remember exact dates and places, but an **association** with other events and dates may often provide the required link with the past. Give the person as much assistance as possible by "jogging" his memory but remember that tact and patience are perhaps the most important qualities of the good interviewer.

Record the statements either on tape or by hand. At a later date review with the person being interviewed what he said. Remember also, that statements should be substantiated with other evidence wherever possible. However, even unverified statements may lead to the use of specific genealogical or historical record sources. No statement should be rejected or accepted without a thorough analysis and evaluation of its veracity.

Personal interviews with relatives do not always produce positive results. They may, however, result in the obtaining of names of other members of the family whom you have overlooked as possible sources of information in your original planning. Such individuals may provide the data you are seeking.

Family Papers in the Home

Personal knowledge is not the only source of genealogical and historical information in the home. There are many documents that may be found in the home and can be of immense value.* Some of these are -

1. Family histories.
2. Family Bibles.
3. Certificates of birth, marriage, and death.
4. Church baptism, marriage, and death records.
5. Journals, diaries, biographies.
6. Old letters.
7. Memorial cards.
8. Apprenticeship records.
9. Military records.
10. Pension records.
11. Scrapbooks.
12. Newspaper clippings.
13. Obituaries.
14. Photographs.
15. Copies of wills, deeds, etc.
16. Citizenship papers, naturalization papers, and passports.
17. Sunday School prizes.

We will consider each of these with special reference to their genealogical and historical value.

1.   Family Histories

It is the happy experience of some to find other members of the family-even persons previously unknown-have spent much time and effort in working on family histories. If the history has not yet been published, the author may still be willing to share this information with you.

2.   Family Bibles

The practice of entering genealogical details in family bibles has long been popular. The quantity of such information in bibles varies. Usually details of the immediate family are recorded, and details of other related families may be shown. It is usual to find the dates of events and names of persons, but places where the events took place are often omitted.

Even in those instances where a family bible is not known to exist, it should always be considered as a genealogical possibility. When you contact relatives, ask if such a bible exists.

3.   Certificates of Birth, Marriage, and Death

---

*The following discussion is adapted from David E. Gardner, C. Derek Harland, and Frank Smith, *A Basic Course in Genealogy*, vol. 1 (Salt Lake City: Bookcraft, 1958) pp. 259-266; now out of print.

Birth, marriage and death certificates are usually prepared at the time of the recorded event. While they generally provide authentic and accurate evidence, you should remember that the information they record was based on verbal statements and may contain errors.

The amount of information on such certificates. See the table at the end of the chapter for precise details of what you can expect to find.

If you find certificates among family records you have saved a great deal of searching and some expense.

4.   Church Baptism, Marriage and Burial Records

Although many of the documents of this type found in the home may be of quite modern origin, there may be those that refer to previous generations. Such records show who performed the ceremony, who the witnesses and godparents were, etc.- information useful in providing background for the story. Again, post-1753 marriage entries may also bear the parties' signatures.

5.   Journals, Diaries and Biographies

The completeness of information from these three associated sources depends on the compilers' methods and thoroughness. Generally speaking, they record movements from place to place and details of births, marriages and deaths. They may give specific dates and places and nearly always contain much valuable information for life histories.

For example, Francis Kilvert (1840-1879) kept a diary of a remarkable quality for nine years. His writings are said to exhibit more human understanding than those of the famous Samuel Pepys. His reason for writing ?

> Why do I keep this voluminous journal? I can hardly tell. Partly because life appears to me such a curious and wonderful thing that it almost seems a pity that even such a humble and uneventful life as mine should pass altogether away without some such records as this, and partly, too, because I think the record may amuse and interest some who come after me.

Here are a few excerpts from those parts of the diaries that still exist, taken from an article in *This England* (Summer 1977):

> Mrs. Pring was married to James Rogers last Thursday as quietly as possible. She would not allow the church bells to be rung, though the ringers entreated her to let them ring a peal, and she openly wished for rain that no one might be able to come to the wedding. Moreover, she invited as few people as possible to the wedding dinner (not even her own mother-in-law) that she might not cause Mr. and Mrs. Venables any needless expense. It was with great difficulty that she was prevailed upon to go to Brecon for the night and let her husband accompany her. Her own wish was that the bridegroom should return to his own house while she slept at the Vicarage as usual. She said she did not want any of that fuss and nonsense. She looked upon marriage as a religious thing. But Mrs. Venables represented to her what a talk would be caused by such a proceeding, so she consented to go as a bride to Brecon for one night and let the bridegroom go too!. . .

7 Sept. 1875: This morning I went to Bath. Having an hour to spare I went into the Catholic Cathedral. I knelt and prayed for charity, unity, and brotherly love, and union of Christendom. Surely a Protestant may pray in a Catholic Church and be none the worse. . . .

27 Oct. 1872: I have rarely seen Langley Church and churchyard look more beautiful than they did this morning. The weather was lovely, and round the quiet church the trees were gorgeous, the elms dazzling golden and the beeches burning crimson. The golden elms illuminated the church and churchyard with strong yellow light, and the beeches flamed and glowed with scarlet and crimson life like the Burning Bush. The place lay quiet in the still autumn sunshine. Then the latch of the wicket gate tinkled and pretty Keren Wood appeared coming along the church path under the spreading boughs of the wide larch, and in the glare of yellow light the bell broke solemnly through the golden elms that stood stately round the church. Today we had one of those soft, still, dreamy, golden afternoons peculiar to Autumn. . . .

When all the people had left the church and no one remained but the Clerk putting away the sacred vessels, I walked alone around the silent, sunny, peaceful churchyard, and visited the graves of my sleeping friends, Jane Hatherell, Mary Jefferies, Anne Hawkins, John Jefferies, George Bryant, Emily Banks, John Hatherell, Limpedy Buckland the gipsy girl, and many more . . .

There they lay all sleeping well and peacefully after life's fitful fevers and waiting for the Great Spring morning and the General Resurrection of the dead. John Hatherell, the good old sawyer, now sleeps in the same God's acre to which he helped to carry the gipsy girl Limpedy Buckland to her burial more than sixty years ago.

Oh, that more of us would record for the future generations our thoughts, our feelings and our hopes !

6. Old Letters

One of the most fruitful of all home sources are letters that were written by various members of a family. These letters, many of which may date back some considerable time, may contain items of family interest, and give valuable information, such as dates and events in the lives of family members. In examining old letters, keep the following points in mind:

1. The writer's name and his relationship to the person addressed.
2. The date and place from which the letter was sent. (This information can usually be obtained from the postmark on envelope.)
3. The address on the letter, which would presumably be the address from which it was written and the home of the writer.
4. The date the letter was written. The date and address establish the writer's residence at a specific time and provide a lead to possible record sources that might provide more complete information.
5. The genealogical and historical contents of the letter.

7. Memorial Cards

The custom of announcing the death of an individual through the medium of a printed memorial card was common to most countries until a few years ago.

In Affectionate Remembrance of

ANN,

Widow of the late John Spencer,

Who died on Friday, July 9th,

Aged 54 Years;

and was this day interred at St. James's Church.

Farewell, dear children, my life is past,
May you and I unite at last;
Mourn not for me nor sorrow take,
But love each other for my sake.

KING STREET, HEBDEN-BRIDGE,

July 12th, 1875.

Such cards were sent to the relatives of the deceased and usually showed the name of the deceased, the date of death and place of burial. Often, other items such as relationships, date of birth and age at death were shown.

8. Apprentice Records

In most European countries, the system of apprenticeship was often the only way a boy could learn a skilled trade. The apprenticeship called for the signing of an agreement between the employer and the apprentice, assuring the apprentice of a thorough training in his chosen profession and giving the employer occupational control of the boy for the length of the apprenticeship, usually seven years. The earlier apprenticeship papers (or **indentures,** as they are often called) usually name the father and may contain other valuable data.

9. Military Records

There are many forms of military records: Records of actual military service, pension records, disablement records, applications for pensions and military bounties, pay books, and pension payment books are only some of the many evidences of military service. The value of these records varies--some show the person's date of birth; others, the name of the regiment; others, the localities in which the regiment was stationed; others, the individual's place of birth and even his parentage. Some merely show that the person concerned did actually have a military background.

Military service medals, ribbons, and photographs may reveal the name of the regiment in which your ancestor served, which in turn can lead you to other military record sources. Once you establish the fact that your ancestor was associated with one of the branches of the services, it can lead to searches in other types of records. Amazing amounts of biographical information can be found in these records.

10. Pension Records

Until recent years, there were few pensions other than those provided for military service. Pension records usually give details of ages or years of birth and sometimes may give the places of birth. An application by the widow of a pensioner for continuation of a pension payment will also usually contain information useful for writing a family history.

11. Scrapbooks

Old scrapbooks kept by families may include newspaper clippings, photographs, pictures of family residences and other miscellaneous items, each of which may provide some clue to places of residence, important events, and other information.

12. Newspaper Clippings

Those items from old newspapers found in the home usually have been kept because they refer to incidents in the lives of members of that family. Notices of births, marriages, and deaths and appointments to important positions are the items most generally kept.

13. Obituaries

Although these generally appear in newspapers, they are listed separately in this chapter, because as the amount of information they give is greater in most cases than that found in other newspaper announements. The date and place of death are usually reported, as well as the names of the survivors of the deceased. The deceased's place and date of birth and even his parentage are often shown.

14. Photographs

Photographs can provide valuable clues for other record searches. The name and address of the photographer may provide a clue to where the family lived. This information may be of limited value, however, since the family could have been away from home at the time the photograph was taken. Names and other details of the people appearing in photographs may be listed on the back and may provide good genealogical clues, leading to searches in other record sources. Photographs of men in uniform may indicate the branch of the service and the regiment in which they served or indicate an association with an organization such as the police force.

15. Copies of Wills and Deeds

Wills and deeds may show the names of relatives and testators, the relationship to them and disclose items of value, such as land and moveable goods--information tremendously useful in writing a family history. They may also include the signature of the testator.

16.   Citizenship Papers, Naturalization Papers, and Passports

These documents vary in the amount of information they contain, but normally they give the person's name, date of birth, and country of origin. They are useful for writing the emigrant part of your family history. Passports often record a precise place of birth although applications for passports are genealogically the most valuable.

17.   Sunday School Prizes

Members of families may have received prizes in the form of books from the Sunday School they attended. Usually in the front of such books are recorded the name of the recipient and the year the prize was given, together with the name and denomination of that Sunday School. The recipient may also have recorded his current address.

The greatest contribution of such a source is that it gives the religious denomination of the Sunday School, establishing the church with which the ancestor was affiliated.

Few, if any, homes will have records of all the types listed in this chapter. However, you should consider everything that may provide a clue. Most of the records found in the home will give information that can be used as the basis for a family group record and will suggest specific searches in other record sources.

It cannot be stressed too much that searching in the home of relatives is an economical way of obtaining information.

One of the most beautiful things about genealogical research in England and writing a history of an English family is the vast amount of material that is available. And just as a good pianist can play beautiful tunes on a piano, so can a person become skilled in the use of English sources and play a beautiful tune with them either in research or in gathering historical detail for a family history.

Following is a list of available sources that can be used both for genealogical research and for family history background. Those available in Salt Lake City, Utah are at the library of the Genealogical Department of The Church of Jesus Christ of Latter-day Saints. The List is expanded from their research paper Series A #1 *Major Genealogical Sources in England and Wales.*

TYPE OF RECORD	PERIOD COVERED	TYPE OF INFORMATION GIVEN	AVAILABILITY	METHOD OF RECORDING	WHO MADE THE ORIGINAL RECORD	RELIABILITY OF INFORMATION
CENSUS RECORDS	1841 and every ten years thereafter except 1941	**1841:** residence, name, approximate age, sex, occupation, indication if born in county-of residence **1851, 1861, and 1871:** residence, name, relation to head of family, marital condition, age, sex, rank, profession or occupation, place of birth (usually by parish and county if born in England, otherwise country of birth only)	1841, 1851, 1861, and 1871 on film (Salt Lake City, Utah) and at the Public Record Office, London. The Public Record Office should be contacted if copies of the enumerations are required for your family history. Remember they are not in your ancestors own handwriting 1891 to present not available for use	An enumerator visited each household These enumerations then went to London and were recopied. The originals were then destroyed.	The "original" we see is the second copying by clerical staff	Affected by mishearing; transcription errors; guesses by the person in the family giving the information; people hiding embarrassing information; guesses at spelling of names
CIVIL REGISTRATION RECORDS	1 July 1837 to present	**Births:** date and place of birth, name, sex, name and surname of father, name and maiden surname of mother, rank or profession of father, name and residence of informant, date of registration. For illegitimate children, often only the name of the mother is given **Marriages:** date and place of marriage, name and surname of bride and groom, ages, marital condition, rank or profession of groom, residence at time of marriage, father's name and surname, rank or profession of father, denomination of marriage, witnesses **Deaths:** date and place of death, name and surname of deceased, sex, age, rank or profession, sometimes relationships, cause of death, name and residence of informant, date of registration	Registrar General, St. Catherine's House, 10 Kings Way, WC2B 6JP, London; local superintendent registrars; indexes 1837 to 1903 on film Salt Lake City, Utah Cheaper to purchase from local registrar if you know the precise place of birth	From information given verbally. You may see the ancestor's signature on his marriage record. Making an X instead of a signature is not necessarily an indication that he could not write. Information supplied is usually by official certificate only	For births and deaths, deputy registrar at the local office. Then extra copies made for distribution Most marriages, because they were performed in Church of England churches, were recorded by the parish minister	As above. The reliability also depends on how the registrar asked the questions

TYPE OF RECORD	PERIOD COVERED	TYPE OF INFORMATION GIVEN	AVAILABILITY	METHOD OF RECORDING	WHO MADE THE ORIGINAL RECORD	RELIABILITY OF INFORMATION
MERCHANT SEAMEN'S RECORDS						As above
Births, marriages, deaths on board British merchant vessels	1837 to present	Names, ages, relationships, dates and description of events. A great deal of biographical information can be gleaned from these records	1837-1874: Registrar General, St. Catherine's House, London. 1875 to present: registers of births and deaths of British nationals at sea were kept by the registrar general for shipping and seamen; these are at the Public Record Office, London	From information given verbally.	Ships officers	All columns not always filled by recorder
Muster rolls for merchant vessels	1747-1851 (Muster rolls prior to 1800 exist only for the English ports of Shields, Dartmouth, Liverpool, and Plymouth)	Usually contain names, ages, birthplaces, places of abode, and details of voyages	On film, Salt Lake City, Utah for 1747 to 1835; originals at Public Record Office, London			
Agreement and Crew Lists	1835-1860	Contain much the same information as the muster rolls	On film, Salt Lake City, Utah; originals at Public Road Office, London	Compiled from other seamen's records	Civil servants	Probable copying errors
Register of seamen's tickets	1835-1856	Name, date and place of birth, and details of career	At Public Record Office	As above	As above	As above

TYPE OF RECORD	PERIOD COVERED	TYPE OF INFORMATION GIVEN	AVAILABILITY	METHOD OF RECORDING	WHO MADE THE ORIGINAL RECORD	RELIABILITY OF INFORMATION
Petitions for Trinity House Pensions	1787-1854	Appications made by old or disabled seamen and their widows for pensions, containing names, ages, details of careers, and information on dependents	On film, Salt Lake City, Utah; originals at the Society of Genealogists, 37 Harrington Gardens, London SW7 4SX	From verbal statements but often supported by documents such as marriage, death, and birth certificates or certified entries from parish registers	Trinity House clerks	Some danger of fraud and forged documents but usually reliable
NAVAL RECORDS General	About 1730-1924	Names, dates, places, births, marriages provide tremendous biographical information, often making it possible to trace a man's career, movements of personnel;	At Public Record Office, London	Logs, journals, official ledgers usually given verbally. Officers often required to present proof of age such as a baptism or birth certificate	Ship's officers and admiralty clerks	Usual errors described previously. Also recorders did not always fill in all the columns provided
Continuous Service Engagement Books	1853-1896	Records of ratings (sailors) containing physical descriptions and a summary of service under each rating; sometimes birthplaces	On film, Salt Lake City, Utah; originals at Public Record Office, London			
MILITARY RECORDS	About 1750-1924	Names, dates, places, births, marriages, movements of personnel; provide tremendous biographical information	Lists of officers in print and on film; chaplains' returns and regimental registers Registrar General's, London; soldier's documents when discharged to pension, 1760-1900, on film; regimental description and succession books, 1772-1874, on film; records of officer's services, 1771-1919, on film; originals of the prior three records, plus the muster books and pay lists, 1760-1878, are at the Public Record Office, London. Films at Salt Lake City, Utah.	As above	Adjutants and clerks	As above

TYPE OF RECORD	PERIOD COVERED	TYPE OF INFORMATION GIVEN	AVAILABILITY	METHOD OF RECORDING	WHO MADE THE ORIGINAL RECORD	RELIABILITY OF INFORMATION
NEWSPAPERS	18th C. to present	Notices; obituaries; announcements of births, marriages, deaths, coroner's inquests, etc. Inquests, notice of achievement, etc. provide much material for a family history	Local custody; British Library Newspaper Library, Colindale Ave., London NW9 5HB, announcements in London Times, 1785-1933; on film, Salt Lake City, Utah	From written and verbal statements	Newspaper employee, relative or friend	Human error but valuable for family history background
POLL BOOKS AND ELECTORS REGISTERS	18th C. to present	**Prior to 1867:** names, addresses, and location of property of freeholders and taxpayers **1868-1917:** names and addresses of all males over 21 years of age **1918 to present:** names and addresses of all males and females over 21	Some in print and some on film (Salt Lake City, Utah); county record offices; public and private libraries; British Library, Reference Division, Great Russell St., London WC1B 3DG; Society of Genealogists, London	County officials prepared list voters	Scribes hired by the lord lieutenant of the county	Clerk errors, printer's errors
CUSTOMS AND EXCISE RECORDS	18th C. to present	Names of officers, various residences of officers, sometimes place of birth and death, details of officers' careers	Some at Public Record Office, London; others at Customs and Excise Office, King's Beam House, Mark Lane, London EC3R 7HE	Detailed ledgers, which make it possible to trace a man's career and movement	Customs and Excise Office clerks	Normally, great care taken
MONUMENT INSCRIPTIONS	18th C. to present	Name of deceased, date of death, age at death, place of birth, some relationships, place of burial	Some in print, some on film (Salt Lake City, Utah); local parish churchyards; town and city cemeteries; Nonconformist cemeteries; private collections	By stoneman or by a copyist	A stonemason, based on a written record	Stonemason could misread his notes. Copier could misread, too, as tones are sometimes in a state of decay

TYPE OF RECORD	PERIOD COVERED	TYPE OF INFORMATION GIVEN	AVAILABILITY	METHOD OF RECORDING	WHO MADE THE ORIGINAL RECORD	RELIABILITY OF INFORMATION
COMMERCIAL DIRECTORIES	1677 to present	Names, places of residence, and occupation of tradesmen; local history; names and exact whereabouts of small localities; lists professional people, and upper-class families living in each parish	Some in print, some on film (Salt Lake City, Utah); local libraries; Guildhall Library, Basinghall St., London EC2P 2EJ; British Library, Reference Division, London; Society of Genealogists, London; publishers of directories	Printed from written and verbal statements	More than likely a printer's clerk	Usually reliable, but tradesmen only listed
ROMAN CATHOLIC RECORDS	1663 to present	**Christenings:** date, names of principal, parents, and godparents **Marriages:** date; place; names of bride, groom, and witnesses **Burials:** date, place, name of deceased	Some in print, some on film (Salt Lake City, Utah); Roman Catholic chapels	Probably in note form or daybook form first and then copied into official registers	Parish priest or his clerk	Affected by mishearing, misleading statements, opinion on spellings, possible loss of notes before official record made
POOR LAW RECORDS	1662-1834	**Parish apprenticeship:** date, names of apprentices and masters, places, occupations, sometimes name of father **Hirings and examinations** (of poor people): age and sometimes place of birth **Settlement papers:** date, names of principals name of parish of prior settlement **Justice's warrants for arrest:** date, name of principal, places; information varies **Removal orders:** date, names of principals, name of parish of prior settlement **Bastardy bonds:** name of illegitimate child's father as well as his mother	Some on film at Salt Lake City, Utah; county record offices; parishes; local libraries. Many lost	On paper, probably from direct questioning	Parish clerks, overseers, justices of the peace	Sometimes questionable because of the very nature of the circumstances being recorded. Very valuable for movements and social conditions

TYPE OF RECORD	PERIOD COVERED	TYPE OF INFORMATION GIVEN	AVAILABILITY	METHOD OF RECORDING	WHO MADE THE ORIGINAL RECORD	RELIABILITY OF INFORMATION
CHURCH, WARDENS ACCOUNTS		**Financial accounts of parish relief:** dates, names of ratepayers and recipients of relief orders from maintenance of soldiers' families (militia) places	Same as parish registers	Financial records on paper or parchment; a matter of book-keeping	Church wardens and parish ministers were automatically involved in caring for the poor, were the overseers of the poor. Any one of these as well as the parish clerk could have made the record	Statements made by the poor may have been exaggerated. Otherwise provide valuable and colorful information for a family history
SOCIETY OF FRIENDS (QUAKER) RECORDS	17th C. to present	Births, deaths, and some marriages; may be somewhat more detailed than parish registers. Minutes include good background information for a family history	Society of Friends, Friends House, Euston Road, London NW1 2BJ; a copy in Salt Lake City, Utah	Most likely assembled from notes and minutes of meetings	Clerks and registrars	Very good
JEWISH RECORDS	17th C. to present	Births, marriages, deaths; names, dates, places, relationships. Records written in either English, Hebrew, or Yiddish	Printed histories and synagogue records	In books similar to parish registers	Clerk of the synagogue, the cantor, or the rabbi	Very good
NONCON- FORMIST RECORDS (MAJORITY OF PROTES- TANT DE- NOMINA- TIONS)	17th C. to present (few prior to 1700)	Christenings and burials similar to parish registers; very few marriages	Many prior to 1837 at Public Record Office and on film in Salt Lake City, Utah; some at local chapels, denominational history societies, county record offices	Similar to parish registers	Secretary, minister, or clerk	Good
BISHOP'S TRANSCRIPTS	1598- 1812; varies beyond 1812	A contemporary copy of parish register entries	Some on film in Salt Lake City, Utah; diocesan offices; county record offices. Some lost	Similar to parish registers	Parish clerk of minister	Sometimes edited; sometimes omit marriages. Valuable to compare with parish registers

TYPE OF RECORD	PERIOD COVERED	TYPE OF INFORMATION GIVEN	AVAILABILITY	METHOD OF RECORDING	WHO MADE THE ORIGINAL RECORD	RELIABILITY OF INFORMATION
PARISH REGISTERS	1538 to present	**Christenings:** date of christening, sometimes date of birth; child's name, father's and sometimes mother's name; sometimes gives place of residence and father's occupation **Marriages:** date of marriage, names of bride and groom, marital condition, parish of residence, sometimes entries of banns **Burials:** date of burial, name of deceased, sometimes age at burial and names of parents	Some in print, some on film in Salt lake City, Utah; local parish custody; some in diocesan and county record offices. Some lost	Early ones recorded in journal-type books. Later ones recorded in bound books of forms	As above, but the original record was often a slip of paper or a day-book entry	Copying errors from original notes do occur. What is recorded is what the recorder heard, which may not have been the truth or may have been misheard. Not every event has been preserved on record
MARRIAGE LICENSES	Bonds: 16th C. to present; allegations: 16th C. to 1823	**Bonds:** cate; name of prospective bride and groom, bondsmen; and notary public; occupations; places of residence **Allegations:** date, names and alleged ages of prospective bride and groom, sometimes present marital condition, occupations, places of residence, and name of father if under legal age	Some in print, some on film in Salt Lake City, Utah; local custody; diocesan and county record offices. Photocopies valuable for family history use.	Directly onto a document that was usually printed, to which the specific details of the intended marriage were added	Surrogate or clerk of diocesan registry	Good because the informants were bonded
SCHOOL AND UNIVERSITY REGISTERS	16th C. to present	Dates; name, age, place of residence of scholars; father's name, sometimes details of birth, place of birth, death, burial. Printed university registers often have additional biographical facts added; valuable in writing a family history	Some in print; local libraries; various schools	Likely copied into school register from a form supplied to the student	The school's registrar	Good

TYPE OF RECORD	PERIOD COVERED	TYPE OF INFORMATION GIVEN	AVAILABILITY	METHOD OF RECORDING	WHO MADE THE ORIGINAL RECORD	RELIABILITY OF INFORMATION
APPRENTICE FREEMEN, AND GUILD RECORDS	16th C. to 19th C.	**Indentures:** dates, names of apprentice, and father master occupation of apprentice **Record books:** dates, names of apprentice and master, sometimes residence **Freemen and guild records:** dates, names of freemen and father's, place of residence, occupation	Some in print, some on film at Salt Lake City, Utah; county record offices; apprenticing of seamen's children 1778-1854 at Trinity House, Tower Hill, London EC3; inland revenue Books of taxes on indentures, 1710-1810 Public Record Office, London; special index 1710-1774 at Society of Genealogists, London and on film at Salt Lake City, Utah; guild and city companies	A standard format was usaully used	Clerk to the guild, company town, parish, etc.	Very good. Modern indexes may have errors
VISITATION PEDIGREES	1500-1650	Pedigrees of families entitled to bear arms	Some in print, some on film in Salt Lake City, Utah; local libraries; College of Arms, Queen Victoria St., London, EC4	Handwritten from what was heard	A group of heralds, by personal visit	Transcribed and printed copies have been added to, sometimes erroneously
CHANCERY PROCEEDINGS	1386-1875	Dates; names of plaintiff, defendant, and witnesses; occupations; places of residence; details of property (real and personal); relationships; some pedigrees	Some printed calendars and original calendars to 1842 on film in Salt Lake City, Utah; some indexes on film also; Public Record Office, London	Handwritten from verbal statements. Provide much background	A clerk in a lawyer's office	Depended entirely on honesty of plaintiff or dependent

TYPE OF RECORD	PERIOD COVERED	TYPE OF INFORMATION GIVEN	AVAILABILITY	METHOD OF RECORDING	WHO MADE THE ORIGINAL RECORD	RELIABILITY OF INFORMATION
PROBATE RECORDS	1380 to present	Provides good family history background **Wills:** name of testator, residence, heirs, relationships, description of land and property, date of will and date of probate, signature, witnesses, executor(s) **Administrations:** name of deceased, residence, name of administrator(s) and sometimes others	Most on film at Salt Lake City, Utah; local custody; calendars only for 1858-1957 on film; probate records, 1858 to present, Principal Probate Registry, Somerset House, London, WC2R 1LP with copies at local registry offices of county record office	By hand, following a fairly general format	Testator, a probate clerk, or a death-bed witness	Good. Relationships sometimes loosely used
QUARTER SESSIONS (CIVIL AND CRIMINAL PROCEEDINGS)	1350 to present	Generally give names, dates, some relationships and important clues as to places of residence and former places of residence. Provide colorful background	Some in print, some on film at Salt Lake City, Utah; county record offices	Sometimes kept as a journal; sometimes a printed form was used	Clerks to the justices of the peace	Depends on information provided by deponents
LAY SUBSIDIES (TAXES)	1216 to 18th C.	Taxes levied by Parliament comprising the poll tax, subsidy tax, hearth tax, and others; these give dates, names, places of residence, and occassionally occupations	Some in print, some on film at Salt Lake City, Utah; all calendars on film or printed (Salt Lake City, Utah); local custody; Public Record Office, London	As above	Parish constables or clerks assigned by county officials	As above
INQUISITIONS POST-MORTEM	1216-1649	Name of deceased, date of death, location of property, name and age of heir and next male in line, name of deceased daughter(s) if no male heir, occasional mention of widow	Some in print in Salt Lake City, Utah; Public Record Office, London	Handwritten, showing lands held, rights under which they were held, and who was heir	An escheator to the crown	Copies were made for the inquest but otherwise should be correct information

TYPE OF RECORD	PERIOD COVERED	TYPE OF INFORMATION GIVEN	AVAILABILITY	METHOD OF RECORDING	WHO MADE THE ORIGINAL RECORD	RELIABILITY OF INFORMATION
MANOR COURT ROLLS	13th C. to present	Dates; names of tenants, manorial officials, jurors; places of residence, relationships	Some in print and on film in Salt Lake City, Utah; local estates; county record offices; local law firms; British Library, Reference Division, London; Manorial Index at Historical Manuscripts Commission, Quality House, Quality Court, Chancery Lane, London WC2A 1HP	Parchment or paper, which could have been copied from notes made at the time the court was held	Clerk to the lord of the manor	Very good
FEET OF FINES	1182-1834	Dates; names of plaintiffs and defendants, places of residence, some relationships	A few in print; Public Record Office, London	Written on parchment, but the document we see probably was drawn up from other notes	Clerk of the court	Very good
DEEDS (FAMILY DEEDS OF LANDOWNERS)	11th C. to present	Dates, names of landowners and tenants, location of property, some relationships, occasional marriage settlements	Some on film at Salt Lake City, Utah; family archives; county record offices; local custody. Calendars to indentures on close rolls, 1574-1860, also on film	Paper or parchment, doubtless from verbal statements	Professional scriveners	Very good
TITHE PAYMENT BOOKS	16th C. to 19th C.	Records of one-tenth of profits payable to the parish minister for the upkeep of the church. Give names and sometimes additional valuable notes. They often give much valuable background for family history	In county record offices and parishes churches. Many now lost	In journal-type books.	The parish minister	Reasonably good, especially for 19th C.

TYPE OF RECORD	PERIOD COVERED	TYPE OF INFORMATION GIVEN	AVAILABILITY	METHOD OF RECORDING	WHO MADE THE ORIGINAL RECORD	RELIABILITY OF INFORMATION
PARLIA-MENTARY PAPERS	Abt 1714-19th C.	Names of people, economic circumstances; but more generally valuable background	Many in print. British Library, London and Library of House of Lords, London, has a complete set. Sets on microfiche now in other large libraries	Through official government surveys	Civil servants	Very good
ECCLESI-ASTICAL RECORDS	16th-19th C.	Names of people who came before the archdeacon's bishop's and archbishop's courts represent a large number of our ancestors	In church registries at the appropriate jurisdictional level Many in print. British library, London, and Library of House of lords, London, have complete sets. Sets on microfiche now in other large libraries	Recorded on paper or parchment	Clerk of the court	Very good
			In church registries at the appropriate jurisdictional level. No indexes available			

Chapter 6

OTHER MATERIALS TO USE IN COMPILING A MULTI GENERATION FAMILY HISTORY

THE RAIN

Did I hear you criticize the rain?
Without it you would indeed complain!
Compare our lush green meadows,
   England's pride,
With barren pastures brown and dried.

Have you ever walked along a country
   lane
and smelled the hedgerows perfumed after rain;
or seen a cobweb hiding in a tree,
like fragile, diamond-scattered filigree?

Has gentle drizzle never brushed your
   face
and melted in a second, without trace;
or a rainbow arched above you in the sky,
a splash of colour pleasing to the eye?

Have you ever seen a country after
   drought,
The people and their cattle moving out?
Attempts at agriculture all in vain,
Did I hear the people pray for rain?

              P. A. HOOSON, *This England* (Summer 1977)

As you can see by reading both volumes in this series, sources to use in compiling a family history are almost endless. This chapter will treat some of the more valuable ones.

Local Histories

Some histories have been written for the smaller than a county English localities, but certainly not enough. You can enquire at local libraries, university libraries and at the Genealogical Library in Salt Lake City, Utah, concerning the possibility of a history for the small locality in which you are interested.

For example, it may be possible for you to locate a book such as *Waveney Valley Studies: Gleanings from Local History,* by Eric Pursehouse (Norfolk, England: Diss Publishing Co., n.d.).

Here are some subject heading from this great book:

    The Great Days of Lopham Linen
    Diss Corsets
    Eighteenth Century Weavers of the Waveney Valley

Diss Weavers
Woolcombers and Worsted Weavers

The Waveney Valley is formed by the Waveney river which flows north east along the borders of Norfolk and Suffolk past Diss, Harleston and Bungay. The author used a variety of sources to glean local history about the people living in the villages in the Waveney valley. My own ancestors came from some of the villages written about in the book. The following excerpts are quoted because doubtless some of my ancestors could have been involved in the making of hemp. Perhaps you could find something written in this book or in another local history about the occupations followed by your ancestors.

Retting was the first stage in the extraction of the valuable fibres of locally-grown hemp. From seed sown in April and May, the plant was ready for pulling in August, when it was tied up in small sheaves or "baits". Hemp stems were hollow, with a "thin bark of fibres" encasing the tender brittle woody part. When retted, or steeped in water, the softened fibrous bark was loosened from the "cambuck", or woody part, ready for the next stage-- "breaking."

It was the practice in some places, notably at Hinderclay and Thelnetham, to "grass" the freshly-pulled hemp or lay it out on a meadow for "dew-retting". This process occupied about five weeks, and necessitated "turning" two or three times a week according to the weather conditions, whereas "water-retting" in ponds was completed in four to five days, depending on weather and temperature of the water. The expert retter could detect the completion of the process, by "feel."

Breaking came next. The "baits" were bundled together and removed to farm barn or cottage shed, where the stems were beaten with a wooden "swingle" to break the wood and detach the fibres, though with larger producers this was performed by passing the stems through a mangle-like machine with fluted rollers.

Scutching followed. It was really the completion of the breaking process, ending in the separation of cambuck from fibre. The former--known as "hemp-offal" was a useful fuel and even a saleable product. The word "scutch" was derived from a Scottish dialect word, meaning to beat or drub.

The raw, tangled fibre was next passed to the heckler, who heckled or combed it into various grades from fine to "tow". The word heckled-- according to an old dictionary of 1842 presented to me by Mr. Ernest Hose, and an invaluable help with these curious words--appeared in several variations: Hickler, higlar, higer, hackler or hatcheler.

The German word was hechel, Dutch hekel, Danish hegle, Swedish hackle, Slavonic hakel--all meaning a "rake". Thus a hatchel, hackle, or heckle was "an instrument formed with long iron teeth, set in a board, for cleansing hemp from tow (the hards or coarse parts) i.e. it was a large species of comb. Some hackles had fine short teeth, others long coarse teeth."

The tangled fibres from the scutcher having been graded by the heckler, were then made up into 14lb. bundles of fine, coarse, or tow, ready for the market or for the spinner--for hemp was sold "by the stone". A good crop of hemp would produce 40st. [560 lbs] of fibre per acre. . . .

The various grades of fibre were next passed to the "spinners"--usually women or children who carried on the work in their homes. It is said that hemp was easier to spin than wool, and that children of five or six years could easily acquire the art--and in fact were taught to spin. Payment for spinning was proportional to the fineness of the yarn produced.

Finally--though most hemp yarn was "woven brown", its natural colour, some was grassed for whitening or bleaching in the sun. While laid out on a meadow, it had to be kept moist.

Thus the stages of processing hemp for weaving were: Pulling, retting, breaking and scutching, heckling, spinning, and grassing.

A detailed study of the parish papers of border villages leaves no doubt whatever as to the importance of hemp growing, and of the trades or crafts to which it gave rise, along the Waveney Valley, from Elizabethan times to the mid 19th century.

Every farm and every cottage with suitable soil grew its patch of hemp, which provided fibres for making so many articles used in everyday life. In fact, next to yeomen, farmers, husbandmen and labourers in husbandry, naturally the most numerous groups in South Norfolk and North Suffolk, workers in "processing hemp" came a very close second. [pp. 158-60]

Surely this is a veritable gold mine of information to use when writing a history of a family native to that area.

Other books cover a wider area than one valley, and others are more specific, dealing only with one village A book of the latter variety recently came to my attention. It is called *The Common Stream: Portrait of an English Village Through 2,000 Years,* by Rowland Parker (New York: Holt, Rinehart and Winston 1975).

It is a tremendously attractive book of 280 pages, and tells the story of the village of Foxton in the county of Huntingdon. If your ancestors were natives of this village, for even one generation or for ten-your work of writing the family history is half completed when you have found this book.

Mr. Parker used a variety of sources to write the history, many of them dealing with individuals. For example, the Church of England maintained its own ecclesiastical courts to punish offenders. In records of these courts are records of people accused of heresy, immoral conduct, failure to attend church, etc.

Almost every person, at some time or another, is said to have come before these courts. There is no index to these court records so searches in them are long and tedious, but if one has the time and the patience they are a very valuable source. Here is a seventeenth century example of this type of record source, taken from pages 173 and 174 of the above named book:

William Yule has not received communion for a year and more.

Elizabeth Awsten of Foxton is vehemently reported to be with childe.

Dorothy Wilson was delivered of a child unlawfully begotten by Richard Carlton of Kings Colledge, as she sayeth.

Mr Meade was presented for not receavinge the Communion at Easter.

Thomas Sturman was reported by his wife that he and Mary Rayner did live together incontinently.

Mr. Brampton (vicar) was presented 'for not catachizinge our Servants nor our Children, neether have wee anie minister Resident in our Parishe'.

Edward Lithell of Melbourn was presented 'for being at Foxton ffayre on the Sabath daye'.

Thomas Campion was presented for begetting his wife with Child before
they were married.

'Neyther the vicar nor his curate doe use the Clokes appoynted for them.'

Andrew Osborn was presented 'for that he had carnal copulacion with his
wife before the daye of their mariage'.

We payne oure Minister as he him selfe saithe is not licenced by his Orders
to preache and yet he preachethe.

Will Breastbone presented for absenting himselfe often tymes from the
Churche.

Nicholas Campion presented for caringe uppon Hallowmas daye.

Thomas Adleson presented for suffering of play in his house ye 29 December
being Sunday.

Wee present Elizabeth - ingeston of this parish for committing fornication
with one John Tomlin as is supposed and as the common fame goeth.

Mistress Meade was presented for goinge out of the church two Sundays
together & being called back by the minister shaked her hands at him &
spake some contemptuous speech against him & so went away.

Books dealing with a town or a village may have pictures of row
houses in which your ancestors lived, or at least row houses **similar**
to them. The example below is London Street, Leek, Staffordshire,
in the nineteenth century and is taken from *Victoria County
History of Staffordshire,* volume 5.

Workmen's dwellings at Wedges Mill, built *c.* 1795

If books like this do not help, look in local libraries, county libraries and county records offices for collections of photographs of people and places. Records of local factories have, in many instances, been moved to county records offices where you can find information on employees pay, the type of machinery used, etc. Such facts and photocopies of the actual documents can add much color to the family history.

Books on Occupations

A good Oxford or Webster unabridge dictionary will provide information on occupations that you have never heard of before. They list many words not used today and give their meanings. Some of these words, such as a corvisor, which is a shoemaker, are described.

There are many books on occupations from which you can draw information for a family history. One excellent example is the four volume series *A History of Everyday Things in England,* by Marjorie and C.H.B. Quennell (London: Batsford, 1960). This series not only shows pictures of people and places but also their occupational implements, drawn to scale. How you use such books will depend on how detailed you wish to make your family history. If your ancestor used a plough in the eighteenth century it might have looked like this. This picture appears in volume 3 of the above series.

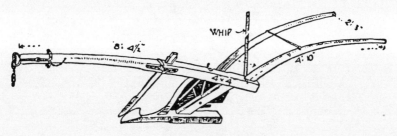

Wooden Swing Plough

If you have London ancestry, this picture appearing in volume 3
will give you an idea of what people looked like and how they lived-
-no wigs, no powdered hair, no fancy clothes. Although London
was the first city to have sewers installed, more than likely the
liquid in which the children are playing is sewer water.

Monmouth Street, Soho, London
An illustration by G. Cruikshank for Dickens' Sketches by Boz

The same volume will help if your ancestor was a wheelwright in the south of England as shown in the accompanying picture.

The Wheelwright's Shop at Beckley, Sussex
After a painting by P. W. Cole

Your ancestor might have operated a well winch as a young man. The boy in this picture, also from volume 3, looks quite well dressed. As stated elsewhere, much of the water was foul, either because the well was not deep enough, the sanitation was poor or the well was a receptacle for dead dogs and cats.

The Well Winch

Through a will you may find that your yeoman ancestor owned a fair amount of land and a farmhouse. This is how the kitchen might have looked in the eighteenth century. This picture appears in the same volume as the preceeding illustrations.

A Kitchen Crane, from a Farmhouse at Biggin Hill, Kent

Many of us today have more than one income. Some of our ancestors did too. They may have had a hand loom in' the house and have been engaged in other work outside. The advantage, of course, of having a loom in the house was that all the members of the family could take turns at the loom. Your ancestor's will might tell if he owned a loom. They were more common in areas where sheep were raised, since in those days sheep were raised primarily for their wool rather than for their meat.

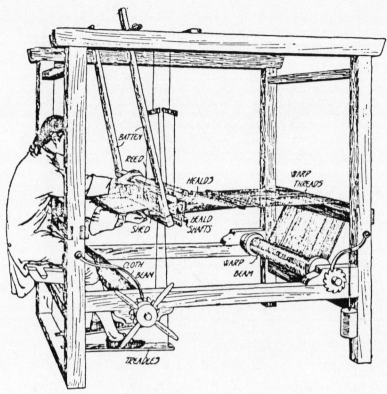

The Hand Loom as used until 1733

Such information is often found in Samuel Lewis's topographical dictionaries. For example, the brief description of Broughton in Furness, Lancashire states-'Previous to the introduction of machinery, the spinning of woollen yarn prevailed to a considerable extent in *private houses*! (*A Topographical Dictionary of England,* 4 vols. [London: S. Lewis and Co., 1831] 1:284; emphasis added).

Another good book on occupations is *Occupational Costumes in England,* by Cunningham and Lucas (London: Adam and Charles Black, 1967). It shows how persons in different occupations dressed. A long list of such books could be prepared. Six other books on English costume are advertised on the cover of this one. Check to see what your own library holds or can borrow for you from another library.

Ploughman. Loose belted jerkin, over-stockings to the knee, boots
with front tab fastening. *c.* 1525.

If your ancestor was a sixteenth-century ploughman, here's how he
might have looked. Note that the caption describes the clothing the
ploughman is wearing.

Cunningham and Lucas back up their own statements with early
drawings and descriptions found in early documents. For example,
they quote from *P. Kalme, Account of His Visit to England...in
1748:*

> The shoes which the labouring man commonly used were strongly armed with
> iron, which followed the shape of the heel and somewhat resembled a horse-
> shoe. [The soles had nails all round and also in the centre.] They sometimes
> had gaiters which were not fastened to the shoes. . .these are strapped
> together on the outer side of the leg.

How tremendously useful as your write your family history!

Here are two examples of seventeenth-century occupations.

Haymakers. Man in shirt, breeches, sugar-loaf hat. Woman in
basqued bodice, long skirt, large hat. 1640-1700.

Joiner wearing shirt and short apron, full
breeches, c. 1688.

I had never heard of a linkboy until I read this book. Linkboys were available in the larger cities and towns to light the way with their torches after dark. They came from poor families, and, the book explains, they very often fell in with bands of thieves to rob the people they were helping.

Linkboy in shirt and ragged breeches. 1747.

In the eighteenth-century housekeepers were copying the dress of their mistresses, says this book. The illustration shows how they looked in 1745.

Housekeeper. Kerchief mob cap and decorative apron, like the informal wear of her mistress. 1745.

During the nineteenth century there were one million domestic servants in service at one time. You will be interested in what they looked like since chances are that some of them were your ancestors. Dress varied depending on the duties of the servant-parlor maid, kitchen maid, footman, butler, etc. *Occupational Costume in England* describes these servants and their dress in detail, as this picture shows.

Parlour maid. Fashionable skirt with bustle; apron; smart cap. 1836-7.

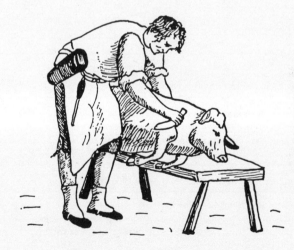

Many ancestors were butchers. Their dress is described in the same book, and could enrich your family history as the picture shows.

Butcher working in shirt, breeches, apron and spats. 1805.

Many millions of barrels of ale were brewed and drunk each year, partially because of the foulness of much of the water available. Beer was given to babes in arms, it being safer than regular drinking water unless the family lived near a clear natural spring.

Thus, there was a great demand for barrels. The man who made the barrels was called a cooper. Quoting from pages 138 and 139 of *Occupational Costumes of England* we read:

Cooper making a barrel, working in shirt sleeves, bibbed apron, brewer's cap and still wearing breeches. 1824.

"A Cooper" in 1640 from the "Cryes of the City of London" is depicted in doublet, breeches, a slouch hat and a leather apron, which protected him from knife cuts and sparks. R. Holme in 1688 describes a cooper thus:

A cooper in his Waistcote and Cap, Breeches and Hose Russet: with an Adds lifted up in his right hand and a Driver [a mallet] in his left, trussing up a Barrel with fire out of the top if it...

Trussing up a barrel = "Putting it together from Boards or Staves within a hoop". Heating the staves of the barrel, makes them "pliable" and "bow to the hoops".

Hogarth in 1751 shows a cooper smoking a pipe outside an inn; he has no coat, his shirt sleeves are rolled up and his apron with a triangular bib is fastened to his shirt button. Tucked into his apron band is a pair of pliers.

All through the nineteenth century the coopers wore aprons (see illustration) with bibs, square or pointed, and by the 1830s the more fashionable trousers were beginning to replace breeches. Jackets were usual, but smocks were occasionally worn and the brewer's cap was very popular.

A **fell** or **felt** is a skin or hide of an animal. So a **fellmonger**, a **feltmonger**, and a **tanner** could be one and the same person.

In most towns the tannery was ouside the walls because of the smell. If there were several parishes within the town or city, the most likely one at which tanner families would worship would obviously be the one nearest the tannery and the nearby workers' houses. A good large map of the town would probably show the location of the tannery and the parish churches.

Feltmonger at tannery. Hide apron over sheepskin apron; leg shields, 1805.

Although there had been mail delivery since the 1600s, it was not until the twentieth century that such a luxury could be afforded by the general populace. *Occupational Costume in England* briefly describes the service over the centuries-inavalualbe in adding accurate background to a history.

Postman in red coat with grey collar and cuffs, blue breeches, white stockings, black shoes and grey top hat. He receives money from lady posting her letter. 1823.

Particularly in the ninteenth and twentieth centuries, thousands of our ancestors were employed as **watermen** on the thousands of miles of canals and navigable rivers.

In the twentieth century the term **navvy** was applied loosely to any laborer who dug ditches or trenches. The word originated during the digging of the vast network of **navigation** canals from 1761 onwards, **navvy** being an abbreviated form of **navigation.** The navvy led a colorful life, working most of the time many miles away from home. For example, in the parish registers of Grove, Buckinghamshire, appears the following burial entry:

29 Jan 1813 Thomas Smith of Sowe, Warws., employed on the Great Junction Canal in which he was drowned, age 18

The following items demonstrate the background that you can find in reference books and record sources in preparing a tremendously colorful story of our watermen ancestors. They are taken from

Population Movements in England and Wales by Canal and Navigable River, Genealogical Research Papers, Series A#5 (Salt Lake City: Genealogical Department of the Church of Jesus Christ of Latter-day Saints, 1968).

Civil registration certificates of birth, marriage, and death and church record entries give clues to canal-oriented occupations such as waterman, lock-keeper, navigator, and others....

Census enumerations will give occupational clues, as may family traditions, old letters, and family documents.

Probate records and marriage bonds or allegations often provide similar occupational clues.

Lewis's *Topographical Dictionaries* indicate if a place lies on or near a navigable river. For example, "Hemel Hempstead: The Grand Junction Canal...passes through Box Moor, within a mile of the town..." Because this out-of-print set of books is now in short supply, abstracts have been made of all such waterway-oriented places and their descriptions, and a copy is available in the Genealogical Society Library...

The [following] example...[develops] the pedigree of a waterman through several generations.

John and Ann Bradley had children christened at Tewkesbury, Gloucester, as early as 1739. Their marriage was not found in this parish, and because of this the search was extended to surrounding parishes. Thirty parishes were searched without success before a decision was made to search the marriage bonds and allegations for the diocese of Worcester (Tewkesbury is in Gloucestershire but near to the border of Worcestershire).

A marriage bond with allegation relating to the above couple was found indicating that they were married at St. John Bedwardine in the City of Worcester by license on 12 May 1738. Additional information showed that Ann's maiden surname was Hiatt, that John Bradley was a *waterman* of Benthall, Shropshire, and a witness to the marriage was a John Harrison, a *waterman* of Tewkesbury.

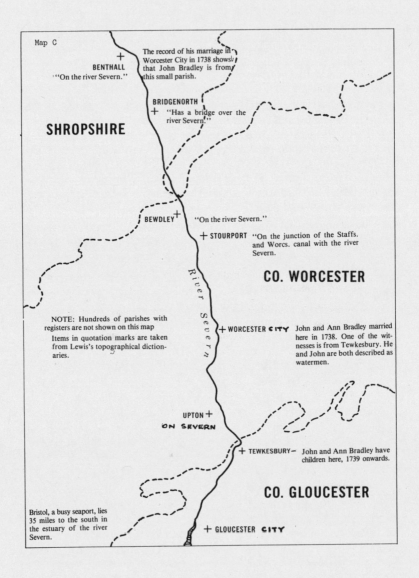

Map C

BENTHALL
✝
'"On the river Severn."

The record of his marriage in
Worcester City in 1738 shows
that John Bradley is from
this small parish.

BRIDGENORTH
✝ "Has a bridge over the
river Severn."

SHROPSHIRE

BEWDLEY ✝   "On the river Severn."

✝ STOURPORT "On the junction of the Staffs.
and Worcs. canal with the river
Severn.

CO. WORCESTER

NOTE: Hundreds of parishes with
registers are not shown on this map
Items in quotation marks are taken
from Lewis's topographical dictionaries.

River Severn

✝ WORCESTER CITY   John and Ann Bradley married
here in 1738. One of the wit-
nesses is from Tewkesbury. He
and John are both described as
watermen.

UPTON ✝
ON SEVERN

✝ TEWKESBURY— John and Ann Bradley have
children here, 1739 onwards.

CO. GLOUCESTER

Bristol, a busy seaport, lies
35 miles to the south in
the estuary of the river
Severn.

✝ GLOUCESTER CITY

A christening of a John Bradley was found at Benthall and accepted as ancestral after the usual eliminating searches in the area disclosed no conflicting information. From the above details, it was possible to trace the movements of the family of a waterman through three counties having navigable rivers before the introduction of canals.

Map C shows parts of the course of the navigable River Severn and gives the locations of Tewkesbury, Worcester and Benthall, and their proximity to the river. From this, it is easy to deduce how John Bradley who was christened at Benthall became a waterman, met his bride further down the river at Worcester, and after marriage reared his family at Tewkesbury which is still further down the river.

My wife's ancestor Thomas Hopkins was also a waterman on the river Severn. He lived in a parish in the bend of the river south of the city of Gloucester. At this point the river is about a mile wide. I visited this area to do research in the church registers. There are no bridges across the river so I was ferried across in a small rowing boat by a local farmer. Further north I was able to take pictures of barges going through the locks on their way to Bristol, just as her ancestors' barge had done.

The knowledge of his occupation becomes genealogically important because he has never been found in the 1851 census returns. He was somewhere along the river Severn or the Bristol Channel on that night.

Parishes and Parish Churches

The ideal way to get information about the parish in which your ancestors lived is, of course, to visit the area and get a feel for it. It is a good idea to study the area first so that the things you see will mean more to you. You will probably want to take many pictures even though industrial development may have changed many things since your ancestors' time.

If you cannot visit the area, you may be able to get information by reading reference books such as those already mentioned or by writing to a friend or relative who lives in the area or even by writing to the parish minister. Nearly all churches carry postcards with views of the church. Fifty cents should cover the cost of the postcard and postage. (Postcard views of the area can also be purchased at the local stationer's store.)

Very often the minister of the parish or a former minister has written a short history of the parish and /or of the church, which may be available at the church or from the minister. For example, I was able to obtain from the parish minister of Rothwell, Yorkshire, a 49-page history of the parish, views of inside and outside the parish church and views of the town. Of particular interest to me was the accompanying picture of the baptismal font, with its elaborately carved, wooden cover. Many fonts had no cover at all, and few as elaborate as this one. But even if this font had no cover it would make no difference to me, because this is where, for several centuries, my ancestors were baptised.

Seventeenth-Century Font and Cover.

Similar books exist for other parishes, depending on the interest of local persons in printing one. For one part of Suffolk, a series of pocket histories was printed in the local newspaper many years ago. These included a picture of the parish church along with a fairly extensive description of the parish. Copies are available in the local County Record Office. Material from such a history is invaluable as background for a family history.

Maps

Modern maps are not as useful as those prepared around the time that your ancestor lived, or at least in the 1800s. *Lewis's Topographical Dictionary of England* (similar dictionaries exist for Ireland, Scotland and Wales) have maps made in the 1830s and 1840s on a county basis. They also made a set not on a county basis which is very hard to find and was the basis for *Genealogical Atlas of England and Wales,* Gardner, Harland and Smith, (Provo, Utah: Stevenson's Genealogical Center, 2nd. Ed. 1974 with index. See page 192.

Libraries and county record offices have a variety of maps that satisfy differing needs.

Burdett's Map of Derbyshire, printed 1791 from surveys made in the 1760s shows the value of old maps. Part of a page is reproduced here. Note the following:

1. The mileage between principal places is given.
2. The large houses, halls, and manor houses bear the name of the owner.
3. Spellings of some places are different from our modern spelling.
4. The letter f is sometimes used for the letter s.
5. Intended canal routes are marked. This was the start of the canal-building period.

Such an excellent map is valuable both for family history and genealogical purposes. Having become familiar with the parts of the parishes from which your ancestors came, you can take an imaginary walk through the area.

Note the 1724 map of Northamptonshire, reprinted in 1974. Each county has its own peculiarities in maps. It is a matter of looking for them.

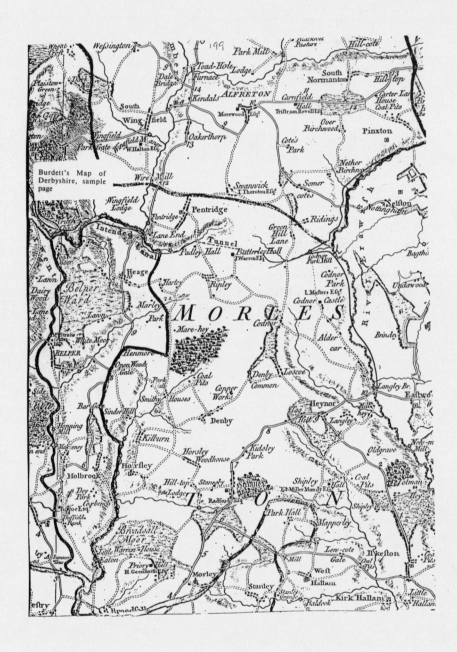

Burdett's Map of Derbyshire, sample page

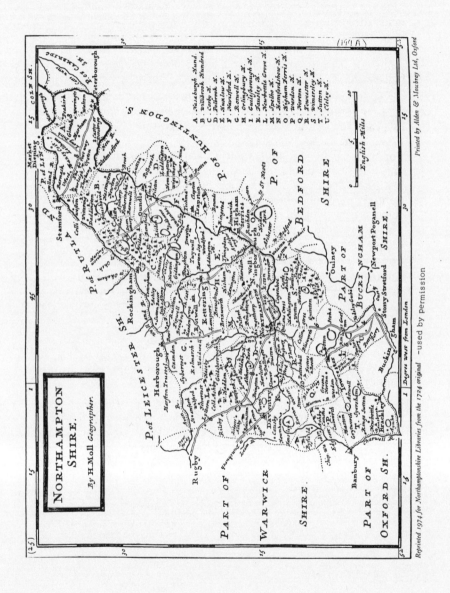

NORTHAMPTON SHIRE.

By H. Moll Geographer.

Tithe maps show the parishes divided into areas for tithing purposes. They are usually to be found in county record offices.

Maps of manorial estates show names of tenants who had strips of land, the position of the strips within the estate and its area (see page 191). What a thrill it would be if you were descended from widow Poole or Phillip Loxley or John Partridge. You could pin-point the precise ground your ancestor worked. The most likely place to find these maps is the county record office.

In addition, there are maps on a county basis that appear in the back of volume 2 of *Genealogical Research in England and Wales* by Frank Smith and David E. Gardner (Salt Lake City: Bookcraft, 1959). Some of these are taken from the 1831 edition of Lewis's Topographical Dictionary, some are hand drawn, showing parishes only. There is also a series of county maps published by the Institute of Heraldic and Genealogical Studied (England) in Canterbury, Kent which show parishes with boundaries, date of commencement of the parish registers and the probate jurisdictions. This series is also published as *Parish Maps of the Counties of England and Wales* (Logan, Utah: Everton Publishers, 1977). See the sample page at page 194.

Another valuable series is the probate jurisdiction maps published by the Genealogical Department of The Church of Jesus Christ of Latter-day Saints, with a table showing which probate jurisdiction to use first.

Ordinance survey maps are available in such detail as to show every street, hill, and vale. The example shown at page 193 is part of the parish of Roade, Northamptonshire. These maps can also be obtained from county record offices.

No one set of maps is absolutely accurate and satisfies every need. Each was made for a specific purpose which may or may not fit an individual need. Reproducing a map from any of these printed sources should be by permission of the publisher.

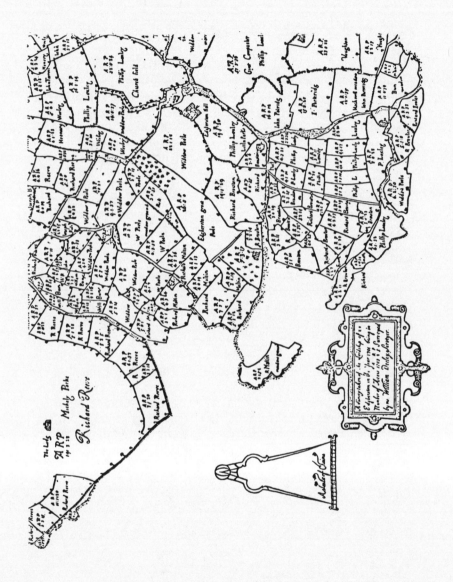

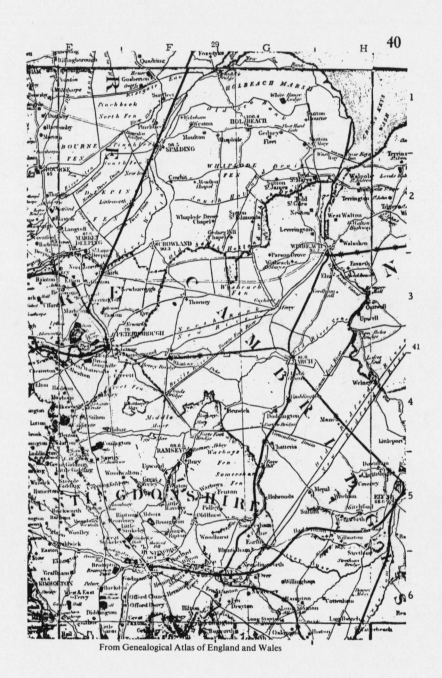

From Genealogical Atlas of England and Wales

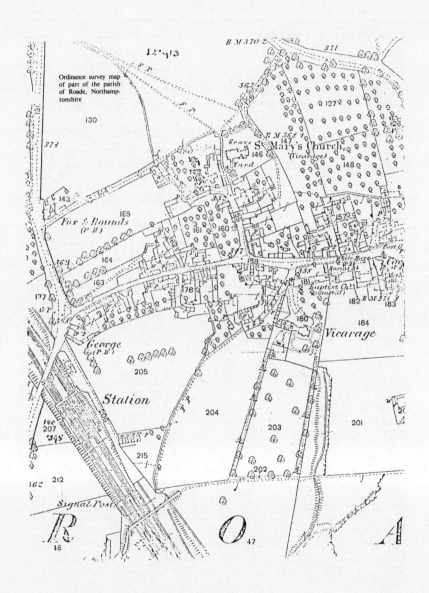

Ordinance survey map
of part of the parish
of Roade, Northamp-
tonshire

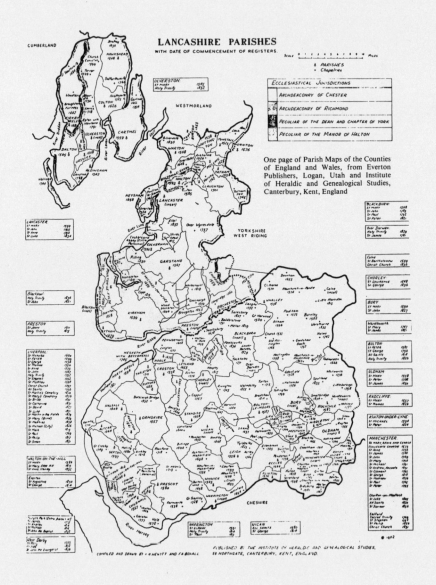

One page of Parish Maps of the Counties of England and Wales, from Everton Publishers, Logan, Utah and Institute of Heraldic and Genealogical Studies, Canterbury, Kent, England

County Record Offices

County record offices are extremely valuable, containing, as they do, so many original records. Add to these records the indexes that interested people have made for much of the material over the years, and you have a veritable gold mine.

Each office publishes guides to its contents, but of course, these publications are never up to date because of the continual flow of material.

Each county record office has its own individual characteristics. These are determined in part by the tax base on which the office is founded, which affects the amount of effort and expense that can go into gathering and tabulating material. A wealthy industrial county is likely to have more tax money for its record office than a poorer county has. The archivist in the wealthy county will be able to afford a larger staff as a result.

A second factor in determining the nature of a record office is the aggressiveness and interest of the archivist himself. Usually he plays a double role--he is both a keeper of ecclesiastical archives and a keeper of civil archives. Despite the archivist's enthusiasm, however, if his office is understaffed he may have records lying uncataloged for long periods of time, because the job is more than one man can do.

Another difference in record offices is the type of records housed. One office may be well known for one subject, and one for another. The types of records one could expect to find in an office are almost endless, ranging from a bunch of personal letters deposited by an individual to a multitude of boxes of papers from some manorial estate hundreds of years old. An office may even have music and copies of popular recordings sung by your great-grandparents. And photographs in county record offices should not go unmentioned. It may be possible to find one for the very street on which your ancestors lived, which has perhaps long since been torn down. (The name of the street may be indicated in a census return or parish register.)

The types of documents that are stored are determined in part by those that are more regularly in demand. Obviously a great deal of attention has to be given to modern documents since they may have to be referred to often. Then again, each staff member may have his "pet" type of document, which he would like to see organized, cleaned, or renovated.

Keep in mind that record offices may have both original and secondary sources, both of which may be valuable. For example, it has already been said that the quarter sessions records for the county and the assize records could almost be classed as the forerunners to the daily newspaper. From these original sources indexes have been made for some areas. From the Personal Names Index at the Essex

County Record Office appear the following entries of the surname Belsham. They provide unusual and interesting background for a family history:

John BELSHAM of Becking presented for keeping an unlicensed alehouse.

..22nd June 1651 John BELSHAM husbandman, Robt. GOODING clothmaker & Geo. ANSELL weaver; Belsham to keep the peace to Lot Kingall of Becking.

..Midsummer 1651. Shalford...."the labourers have done their work...Abraham Belsham with his cart 1½ days...John BELLSHAM with his cart half a day.

19th Dec. 1689 Caleb MEASANT & John FLANNER, both of Earls Colne, yeoman; Measant to answer Margt. Pennocke touching his coming into her house with John LAMBERT, & Jos. BELCHAMP in a riotous manner & taking her goods by virtue of a pretended levy out of County Court.

Joseph BELCHAMP 3rd August 1698 Assaulted by Henry DANIAN who stole his purse, key and money at Saffron Walden.

Joyce Belcham, 1677, of Stebbing, refused to work.

Mary Bekham. Felsted 1650....3 men to keep the peace to Mary Belcham wife of John Belcham of Felsted, miller.

9th July 1632. Thomas BELCHAMP Defaulter on work with his cart-6 days behind.

...1650. Thos. BELCHAMPE of Great Coggeshall, husbandman before & since 12 Feb. 1649 kept a common alehouse there without a licence.

20th Feb. 1696. Wm BELSHAM labourer & Rich. MOSIER, yeoman both of Tillingham to answer at the first sessions after Sarah Coleman should be delivered of a bastard. Owes 2s.

Such an idex may not be found in another county record office. It is well to study the card indexes to the various holdings in each office even though there may also be printed guides.

One final but important difference: Many county record offices have shorter opening hours than others, a sore point with visitors who may have traveled a long way and wish to make every minute count.

Thus each office has its own individuality. But be assured that most are full of sources that can add both fact and color to your family history.

In addition to county record offices, there are special offices that house more specialised collections. For exampie, there are special newspaper collections, special repositories for old music. In short, some things that are national in scope may be found in places other than in county record offices.

Museums

A veritable gold mine of working models or period clothing, coins, stamps, and a hundred other things is the museum. Most museums sell picture post cards of the more attractive items. The Science Museum in Kensington, London, gives all kinds of glimpses into the past. One could spend several days there. This is also true of many such institutions.

County Histories and Topographical Dictionaries

Many county histories and topographical dictionaries have been written. The best series of county histories is the Victoria County Histories series. This series has been in progress for many years. Where a county has been finished there are several large volumes, going into much detail. For some counties only certain volumes are ready.

Topographical dictionaries and commercial directories also provide details of parishes and counties, but as a rule they are not as valuable as the Victoria County Histories series. For example, for the parish of Brampton in Huntingdonshire, Lewis's *Topographical Dictionary of England* had about a quarter of a page description; the commercial directory for the county had less than a page; the Victoria series had eight large pages of description plus eight pictures, showing the inside and outside of the parish church and other large and important buildings.

Use of such materials can add tremendous color to a family history.

Histories of Schools

If you know that your ancestor went to a certain school, look for a printed history of that school. There are many such histories available. You will learn what the curriculum was at different periods, the hours of attendance, names of headmasters, and perhaps even incidents that occured while your ancestor was there. Perhaps you will find that a certain headmaster was rather harsh; perhaps that your ancestor was flogged. Some authors go to a lot of trouble gathering such interesting information from school board minutes.

Books of a Miscellaneous Nature

A popular series, though not currently printed, are the Notes and Queries published for various counties. For example, on page 196 of *Northamptonshire Notes and Queries* appear details of the disbursements for the joint parishes of Roade and Ashton for several years:

Sept. 1. Expenses about casting bells which I paid at Lovells . . .   0 2 0
Dec. 28. Given a woman that had Small Pox to nourish her and
her two children 0 0 2
1723. This year we pay double cess money
                                                J. Thicknesse, Rector.
1727. Oct. 25. Given to 2 women who had a very great loss by
fire, their husbands burnt and their houses burnt by some
men who robbed them; and two of their children was burnt
and their maid killed
1727-8. Jan. 20. For relieving a Souldier that was under Col.
Montagu and served thirty years and had a printed pass; had
a wife and 3 children and no money to pass their night's
quarters. Charges with relieving them 0 0 6

The levy for 1730 is given at full, sir Halland Egerton paying £ 3 2s. od., being more than double the whole of the rest of the payments. The duke of Kent is entered as paying 4s. The account closes this year with a balance of 12s. 6d. due to the incoming constable.

If your ancestors were from these parishes, even though they may not be mentioned, chances are that the people who are mentioned knew your ancestors. Using some imagination, you could fill in many details about your ancestors' lives from these records.

It is worth determining if there is such a series for your particular county.

Modern Photography

Photographs are almost unnecessary to mention, but they play a valuable part in any family history. A skilled photographer can be helpful in photographing an old, worn-out tombstone, or the outside and inside of a church when a ready-made copy is not available.

True, your ancestral home may have been pulled down, but what stands there now? Although the street on which your ancestors lived 150 years ago still exists, it is different now. But how it looks now is better than nothing at all. Furthermore, what now are modern photographs will not be modern 50 years from now, when your grandchildren are reading the history.

Much information can be found by aerial photography. I have a book called *The Lost Villages of England,* by Maurice Beresford (William Clowes and Sons, 1954). It recounts the discovery of the sites of villages that were abandoned during the period when it was more profitable to enclose whole areas for sheep raising than to farm the land. Although wheat now grows where the villages once stood, the outline of the villages can be seen when the sun is in the right direction.

Final format for a multi-generation family history

This is a personal preference but I have found the following format to be attractive in the family histories I have written:
1. The whole history should be written simply and in an attractive style to appeal to young people.
2. The title of the book superimposed on a map of the county or other area. If a principal occupation is known for the family some occupational picture could also be superimposed on the title page, e.g. a hand weaving loom.
3. A signed message to future generations from one of the older family members or from the president of the family organization.
4. A two or three page description of England with a map of England, especially if the history is being written for a United States family with United States descendants.
5. Suitable selected verse about England.
6. Description of the county or counties where the ancestors

lived, illustrated with maps and pictures.

7. Description of the parishes in which the ancestors lived, also illustrated with pictures.

8. Now you are ready to tell the ancestral story. Go back to the earliest known generation and work towards the present, until at least the family left England. Draw a brief sketch pedigree of that generation like this:

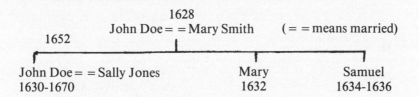

1628

John Doe = = Mary Smith   (= = means married)

1652

John Doe = = Sally Jones   Mary   Samuel
1630-1670   1632   1634-1636

(all children were christened in the parish church at. . . . .)

It is not necessary to show complete dates here if these already appear in another part of the family's records.

Then describe the social, historical and religious conditions of that generation in that part of the country or in the nation as a whole. Illustrate well with pictures of events, people, occupational dress, tools, houses, etc., using the type of books described earlier in the chapter.

Repeat this process through each generation as you come forward to more modern times. If possible and practical add photocopies of the original entry in parish registers or bishop's transcripts of direct line christening, marriage and burial registers. Add photocopies of birth, marriage and death certificates where the event took place after 1 July 1837. Add copies of pertinent wills together with a transcription of the wills. Photocopies of marriage bonds and allegations and census enumerations can also be used and add much flavor to the total product. Finally you may wish to add a sketch pedigree comprising all the ones you prepared for each generation. To simplify it, you may wish to retain only the direct ancestor in each generation.

Printing the Family History

For large wealthy family organizations it is a relatively simple matter to turn the manuscript over to a printer or publisher. Bear in mind that large quantities are cheaper per copy than small quantities.

You may wish to get bids from several firms, including bids for several different quantities.

For small quantity printing, say anything from one copy to 100 copies, it is more economical to use a xerox copier approach. There are now copying machines on the market that produce excellent black and white copy from the typescript and handle black and white pictures quite well, too. There is also a new multi-color xerox copier for the pictures you wish to reproduce in multi color. These are much cheaper to reproduce than by the regular photographic process. A few color pictures will greatly enhance the looks of the finished history.

Binding can be done quite economically by using the plastic comb, or metal rings, plastic rivet or staple and tape.

Thus, you need not be talking about hundreds or thousands of dollars to print an attractive family history.

The final and perhaps the most difficult step is to get the younger generation to read it. Family get togethers are good settings. Show and tell at school is another good approach. Family history classes in schools when they develop, as they will, on a larger scale than at present, will also help.

EPILOGUE

This book no doubt will affect different individuals in different ways. Some may be motivated to do only a cursory job. Some may be controlled by lack of time and funds. A good, active family organization can play an important part here, supporting some one or more persons with the funds necessary to do a good job. The family or the individual should decide how thorough the family history is going to be. They may decide that for the present, they will concentrate on the paternal surname line only. They may decide to write the history briefly, fairly well done, or very well done. Later they may decide to go more deeply into the history of that line. Or they may decide to go to the maternal line.

But whatever your goals, hopefully you have found, in the foregoing, and in volume 1 of the same series, sufficient motivation to start off on the family history trail. There is no question that the better the job we do in writing these histories, the greater the effect they will have on our children and grandchildren as they examine their roots.